never
too late

amber portwood

WITH BETH ROESER

never too late

A POST HILL PRESS BOOK

A POST HILL PRESS BOOK

ISBN: 978-1-61868-959-7
ISBN (eBook): 978-1-61868-960-3

Never Too Late
© 2014 Amber Portwood with Beth Roeser
All Rights Reserved

Cover design and photography: Travis Franklin
Interior design and typesetting: Neuwirth & Associates, Inc.

Post Hill Press
109 International Drive, Suite 300
Franklin, TN 37067
posthillpress.com

I owe this all to my baby, Leah.
Without her, I don't know where I would be today.

contents

contents

never
too late

1

What Happened?

You remember when the bell rang on the last day of school before summer vacation? That explosion of freedom you felt? If you could multiply that by a million, you still wouldn't be close to the joy of walking out of prison after seventeen months of being locked inside.

Seventeen months. I was twenty-three years old and I'd been in prison for seventeen months. Other people my age were getting used to life after college, hanging out with friends, finding jobs, and building their futures. And here I was, Amber Portwood, age twenty-three, a single mom, recovering drug addict, and MTV reality star, walking out of freakin' prison after serving seventeen months.

What the hell happened?

How does a regular girl end up in a situation like that? Or had I ever *been* regular? How did I get so far away from the kind of life I meant to have? What was going through my head when I made the mistakes that brought me here?

It's a complicated story, I'll tell you that much. But thanks to those seventeen months in prison, I had had a lot of time to think about the complicated things. Every night for over a year, I lay awake in my bunk staring out the window, just thinking. The lights in the yard were so bright I couldn't even see the night sky. I just lay there alone and stared at nothing, going deep into my thoughts and trying to understand who I was and what I had done to my life.

Those nights changed me in a real and serious way. They made me figure out who I really was and what I needed to do. And that gave me the focus I needed to put my heart and soul into changing myself for the better and getting out of that hellhole. You're not living in a normal way when you're locked up. You feel like you're barely living at all. Physically and emotionally, you're trapped in there just knowing that nothing you do really matters until the day you get out. And that's if you're lucky enough to be getting out. So what do you do with the time until then? You can drag yourself through it like a jailhouse zombie. You can let it beat you down. Or you can do what I did, use that time alone at night and take a long, hard look at what got you into the situation in the first place, and how you're going to repair all the damage that's been done.

When I walked into that prison, I had a drug addiction that seemed completely invincible. One minute I was earning money and fame being featured on MTV's *16 & Pregnant,* giving birth to a daughter, and learning to be a teenage mom on camera. The next minute I was swallowing ungodly handfuls of prescription pills and losing myself in a haze of drugs as my life fell into pieces around me. My family fell apart. I lost custody of my daughter. The worse things got, the more pills I took. Nothing could make me stop. Two months in rehab, three months in jail, criminal charges, probation, drug court, and suicide attempts—none of it even made a dent in my addiction to pills. As the MTV cameras rolled, I was on a secret mission to destroy myself. I didn't just go downhill fast. I motorcycled off a cliff.

The people who followed *16 & Pregnant* and the spin-off series *Teen Mom* are familiar with a lot of the main events in my story, not just from watching the shows but from the endless tabloid coverage they brought me. For some twisted reason, my life as seen on MTV became part of the entertainment news cycle, and sometimes it felt like half the world was watching me mess up. They watched as I struggled with anxiety and depression in the months after I had my daughter, Leah, and they saw me get my first prescription for Klonopin. While I wrapped myself in a cloud of painkillers and sedatives behind the scenes, audiences watched my world fall apart on the surface. The tabloids kept a close eye on me as my life exploded in one disaster after another: custody drama, battles with CPS, and fights between me and Leah's father. There were even cameras in our home when one of our fights turned physical, a television moment that shocked the media and the public and eventually caused the court to press charges against me for domestic battery. To the outside world my life looked like a tornado of tears, anger, and ugly fights, and I looked like an irresponsible, immature kid with an uncontrollable temper, not fit to be a mom.

But the reality was even darker than what people saw on screen. By the time *Teen Mom* was done, I was stuffing myself with insane amounts of prescription drugs, from anxiety medications to heavy-duty painkillers. I took myself to the edge of death with the amount of pills I swallowed, and that was only after I destroyed my relationships with friends and family to the point where there was nothing left but me and my addiction.

I walked out of prison knowing it had saved my life.

But still, I'd been there long enough. It was time to get the hell out of there and throw myself into getting back as much as I could of what I had lost. I had to believe that was possible, and I did believe it, with all my heart.

My mom, brother, and nephew all came to pick me up from prison, and I'd never been happier to see them. I walked into their arms trying to play it cool, even though inside I was freaking out. Inside, I was doing the whole movie scene thing, falling to my knees and screaming for joy, kissing the ground or doing cartwheels. But on the outside, I didn't know exactly how to act. In prison you're always being watched, and you learn to carry yourself a certain way. It's a different world with different people in it, and you adapt to it in ways you don't even realize until you get outside. You have to adjust to the normal world again. It takes a while to let it sink in that you can spend the rest of your day—and your week, and your month, and your life—however the hell you want to. That's a crazy change in lifestyle, and I was kind of reeling as I took it in.

There was one thing I wasn't uncertain of at all. When I got in the car with my family, I had my sights set on seeing my daughter, Leah. I was so excited to see her I wanted that car to hit warp speed. During the entire seventeen months I was in prison, I only saw my daughter three times. The first year, I didn't see her at all. It was the most painful thing about being behind bars, and you better believe that every night I spent crying in there, I was crying over my daughter. But missing

Leah was also what motivated me. I knew the worst effect my addiction had on my life was the distance I let it put between my daughter and me. So I worked my ass off to change myself in prison, to learn and grow and take control of my life so that I could get back to being a mother to my daughter. Now I had entered the next phase of that mission, the real phase, and I couldn't wait to see her and start the rest of our lives as a family.

Even though I had my mind set on the road ahead, as we drove away from the prison, I couldn't help looking back with a bittersweet feeling. As happy as I was to be out, it killed me to think of the women I knew who were still inside and had no chance of seeing their own children anytime soon. Not everyone back there was a saint, and there were some real bitches in the mix. But I'd gotten to know so many women in prison who were just like me and whose lives and experiences became a part of the lessons I learned there. I found true friends among those women, people who were by my side literally morning and night during one of the most difficult and lonely experiences of my life. They witnessed my struggle to change and all the determination I put into it, and they were the first ones to see the difference. My friends inside watched me make the difficult transformation from a drugged up mess into a person who was more clearheaded, calm, and focused than anyone would have thought possible. Many of those women were on journeys of their own. They had kids on the outside, too, and other relationships they had either lost or were struggling to hold onto. I wasn't the only one trying to change in there, and I wasn't the only one strong enough to do it. As a community, we helped drive each other and lift one another up through that struggle. Without that part of the experience, I wouldn't have come anywhere near as far. So I held those women close to my heart, and I owed them a lot.

Now that I had left those walls, though, we wouldn't be allowed to have any contact with each other. Some of them would stay in prison for many more months, some for years, separated from their families and feeling further and further from the real world every day. It was heartbreaking, and it made me feel truly blessed to have my freedom and the ability to see my daughter again.

Those were things I couldn't take for granted. The path back to prison was still open behind me, I knew, and I wasn't going to be stupid and fool myself into thinking I could never end up back there. It was only a matter of time before I would have to face the temptation of abusing drugs again. Getting out meant I had the freedom to make my own mistakes. And I knew how devastating my mistakes could be.

My choices and actions had hurt the people around me badly, from the way I changed because of my drug addiction to my sudden and drastic decision to choose serious jail time over rehab. I'd left a lot of confusion and disappointment behind. But during my months alone in prison I came to understand that it's never too late to turn things around.

And it was like fate wanted to prove that to me the day I got out of prison. When my mom, brother, nephew, and I finally stopped somewhere to get a bite to eat, I got the greatest surprise I could have possibly gotten when I found my father standing in the restaurant.

All of my effort to stay composed totally fell apart when I saw my dad standing there, with the rest of my family so close by. He didn't live nearby anymore, and he'd been dealing with serious illness for years. So it had been a long time since I'd seen him, and it had been many years since my parents, my brother, and I were together in the same room. Between the four of us, there were a lot of incredibly painful memories, hurt feelings, and difficult disagreements. But that day was actual proof that it's never too late for a family to get back to a place of love and affection, no matter what's gone down between them during harder times.

That day I felt like it was more obvious than ever how much my father and I had in common, just in terms of the mistakes we'd made and the things we'd gotten into. His alcoholism destroyed his relationship with my brother and me, to the point where we hated him as teenagers. But when it seemed like nothing could ever repair the damage his behavior had done, he was able to apologize and turn his behavior around, and we were able to forgive him. Now here we were together as a family, able to look at each other with real love and fight together to move forward. Years ago, my father had taught me a lesson I took a long time to understand. It was that it's never too late to turn things around. No matter how low you think you've sunk, no matter how many bad things you've done, or how much damage you think you've done to your life, it's never too late to change.

◆

That night I took a long bath and laid down in bed feeling like I was in heaven. From now on I'd be living with my grandmother, sticking to a quiet life, and focusing on getting on my feet and maintaining my sobriety. And whenever I could, I was going to see Leah. I couldn't wait.

This was the way it was supposed to be. No pills, no rehab, no fights, no jail. It didn't seem so hard, did it? So how was it, exactly, that I'd wound up way the hell off course? Where exactly had I gone wrong? What had I been thinking? And now that I was out, could I really turn it all around?

Like I said, it's a complicated story, and there's a whole lot more to it than what made it past the editors at MTV. The craziness of my life didn't start when the cameras came. By that time, I had already experienced more danger, drama, and heartbreak than the producers had any way of knowing about. Being pregnant was a big deal, but it was only the latest drastic event in a life that had already taken many strange turns.

Addiction. Mental illness. Death. Divorce. Betrayal. Violence. Suicide attempts. Felony charges. Rehab. Drug overdoses. Jail. Oh yeah, and there's some sex and rock 'n' roll in there, too. But I'm going to tell you how it all happened. Maybe when I'm done, you'll understand some of the weirder parts of the story, like the reason I walked away from my daughter to voluntarily serve time in prison.

But I hope you'll understand something else, too. Because as far as I'm concerned, this isn't a story about how I fucked up and hit rock bottom. It's about how I found myself when it seemed like I was completely lost. It's about how I repaired what seemed completely destroyed. It's the story of how I learned that it's never too late to live a different way, no matter what you've done.

And it's not just a story about me. It's about all the people I've learned from in my life. People like my brother, who stood by me and never gave up no matter how far gone I was. People like the women I met in prison, who showed me how a loving community can help you find the strength to stay on your feet. People like my father, the first person to prove to me that it's never too late to make a change, do the right thing, and be there for the people you love.

Everyone makes mistakes. Some of us make really, really big ones. But the biggest mistake of all is thinking nothing will ever get better. It is never too late to make things better.

How do I know that? You're about to find out.

2

How to Make and Break a Family

The best place to start a story is usually the beginning, but sometimes that's easier said than done. It might sound crazy, but I don't remember much about my life when I was really young. I've blocked a lot of it out. Now, I'm not saying I had the worst childhood. It wasn't the best, but I remember some good times with my mom and dad and my big brother, Shawn, or as I still call him, Bubby. Definitely, there were good times. It's just that those good times are overshadowed by other times that were truly terrible.

Things were never easy for my family. There wasn't much money, and my mom and dad worked all the time to keep food on the table. It didn't make it any easier that both my parents struggled with addiction. My dad's partying and drinking was the main reason we moved from Florida to Indiana when I was just a baby. Down there he'd been kind of a wild child, and even after my brother and me were born there were a lot of clubs and bars and parties that made it hard for him to settle down and focus on his new family. It's clear looking back that these kinds of issues were always an influence on our life. Addiction was always hanging over us, along with all the struggles and fighting that went with it.

But my parents tried their best to do things right. They thought things would be better in Indiana, where it was quieter, and for a while they were. We didn't have a lot of money, but we did okay. My mom was a waitress, and my dad worked in construction. They were always working hard, long hours, for as far back as I can remember. Our parents took good care of us, the very best they could. A few years after the move, my mom even had another daughter, Candace.

The first thing I remember when I think about those days is what a total daddy's girl I was. I loved my dad so much. Some of my best memories from when I was little are of hanging out with him, listening to his records, getting my first exposure to bands like Heart, ZZ Top, and Guns N' Roses. I love thinking about how he used to braid my hair in the mornings. My dad was my hero. We had a special bond from the very beginning, and I bet if you asked anyone who was there at the time they'd tell you what a beautiful relationship we had. I was so young that I can't remember much more than those kinds of dream-like memories of hanging out with him on sunny days, the little-kid snapshots I have in my mind of us spending time together, laughing and hugging. But now that I'm older I see even more clearly how much I take after him, and I wonder if it was obvious back then. I imagine when the two of us were sitting around rocking out together to those records, we looked like two peas in a pod.

Those memories are bittersweet, though. Because we didn't have all that much time to be happy together, me and my brother and sister and parents, before it all fell apart.

I was only four at the time, but I remember that night so clearly it's like it's a movie in my head. We were living in these apartments in Anderson, Indiana, and I was lying on the bottom of the bunk bed I shared with Bubby. Candace was sleeping in her crib down the hall, and our dad was watching TV in the living room. It was really late when my mom came home, said hello to my dad, and went in to check on her youngest daughter.

She must have known almost right away that something was wrong.

All of a sudden my brother and I heard this horrible screaming. It scared us so bad we jumped up out of bed and ran to find Mom and Dad. We could hear them in the other room with Candace, and my mom was yelling, "She's not breathing!"

When we got to the door of that room, we saw our parents living out their worst nightmare. Candace was in my father's arms, and he was trying to give her mouth to mouth. The details of that scene are so clear in my mind, and so horrifying, it turns my stomach to think about it. I try not to. But I can remember exactly what she looked like in their arms. I can remember people from the building rushing into the room and someone bringing in a stretcher.

Candace Ann Portwood had only been my little sister for two weeks.

Sudden Infant Death Syndrome is what they call it when a healthy baby just passes away without any apparent reason. I don't even think there are words to explain what SIDS does to a family. Bubby and I were so young—he was only seven or eight at the time—there was no way we could fully understand what happened. But the really awful thing was nobody understood. People still don't know what causes SIDS or how to prevent it, and back then it was an even bigger mystery. Everybody wanted to blame someone, and pretty soon they decided to blame my dad. Maybe it was because he was the one who was with us just before my mom came home and found Candace lying there, not breathing. Or maybe his alcoholism made him an easy target, made people think he wasn't a responsible father. Either way, it wasn't right to lay that kind of blame on someone for the death of their own child, and in the end I think it made it basically impossible for our family to recover.

I can't even imagine how horrible it must have been for my parents, but they tried their best to help us kids through it. My mom tried to explain it to me. I remember her sitting on my bottom bunk while I walked around the room by the closet and the rocking horse. I asked her why my little sister had to die. What could she have said? I don't even remember, but I hate to think about how hard that conversation must have been for her.

I remember the funeral for Candace, the little coffin and the headband she wore.

Years later, when I had Leah, my memories of that night came back stronger than ever and haunted me in the worst way. I used to sleep with my daughter's crib right beside my bed, just so I could wake up and make sure she was still breathing. Sometimes she'd be sleeping so deep and breathing so lightly that I'd get scared and put my fingertips under her nose to check. If that still didn't make me feel better, I'd have to pick her up just to hold her in my arms and make sure she was still alive. Leah's way too old to be at risk now for what happened to Candace, but that feeling still makes me cold with fear inside.

I was so young when we lost my sister, and I remember I was so stunned that I couldn't even cry at the time. I didn't even understand death. But the whole horrible thing has just stayed with me, and now that fear I felt with Leah makes me cry when I remember. It breaks my heart now that I'm old enough to understand what my parents went through. What could be worse than losing your child? As a mother I can't wrap my mind around it, and I don't want to. It doesn't shock me as much now, looking back with that adult-level understanding, that my family fell apart the way it did. If my parents had struggled before, they didn't stand a chance against something like that.

♦

After Candace died, my family started to deteriorate. That was the start of the bad times that turned into a blur in my memory. Still, I don't have to remember everything perfectly to reach some kind of understanding of what happened. Most of all, it's obvious that being blamed for Candace's death was more than my father could bear. Can you imagine a heavier burden than that?

It's still so odd to me that people could be so cruel that they'd lay that on his head. I wish I could have been older then, and maybe I could have stopped it from happening like that. But pretty soon he was blaming himself, and his alcoholism went out of control. What do you expect? How could anyone cope with the guilt and shame of being blamed for the death of their own child, let alone someone who already struggled with addiction?

Of course my mom had her problems, too. She drank. He drank. They were both devastated by what had happened and completely miserable with each other. It was a perfect recipe for an unhappy home. There were no happy years of marriage in the cards for them from that point. For the rest of their time together, they were fighting and screaming all the time.

And I mean *all* the time. When I was growing up there wasn't one single day in our house where my parents weren't fighting and screaming and cussing at each other. I can remember my brother and me running out of our room at night and yelling at them to please stop, please stop, telling them we had school in the morning. But they never would. They fought every single night about anything and everything. I mean, stupid things!

It was in that environment that I first experienced the power of addiction to damage even the strongest relationships. Remember how I said I loved my dad when I was little? How I was a total daddy's girl? I was barely in grade school when that stopped being true. My father was absolutely horrible back then. The combination of all that pain with his drinking problem just turned him into a different, horrible person. When he and my mom were fighting he'd scream the most awful things at her, calling her names and acting vicious. Before long, he was doing it to me, too. The things I grew up listening to in that house were just terrible. Day after day, year after year, I had to learn to live with all that violent screaming, anger, and meanness. It was always happening around me, for no reason, with no point and no end.

By the time I was in grade school, I hated my father. All my early memories of the rock 'n' roll records and the hair-braiding were replaced by what came after that: my father the mean drunk.

We ended up moving out of those apartments and into a better place, but it came with a big problem: it was next to a bar. So my mom was always going over there and screaming at my dad, dragging him home, and screaming some more. But she had her problems with drinking, too. She wasn't some sloppy, fall-over drunk or anything. In fact both my parents somehow kept working constantly through all of this. But when she was waitressing, she'd drink on the job. Then she'd come home, and as soon as they were together it was screaming and fighting again, at the bar next door, in the house; it didn't matter. Screaming, screaming, screaming! Even when we tried to do fun stuff, like going to Disneyworld, there was always that stupid, horrible drama. I don't remember one single day without it.

So, yeah. My childhood wasn't the worst, but my home life sucked. It really did. There's a lot I wish had been different. I wish we'd had a peaceful house, with parents who got along and weren't drinking and screaming all the time. I wish I wasn't begging them to get divorced when I was in kindergarten. And I wish we hadn't lost my baby sister.

But there's one thing I can say about my family, even if it doesn't make sense to anybody who wasn't there with us: they always tried to get better. They did the best with what they could. Even my dad, I don't hate him for those bad times. Knowing him now, and what a big heart he has and how much I'm like him, I don't blame him for falling apart. If that happened to me—it's hard to even think about it—but if Leah died and no one could tell me why, and they blamed me for it? I'd do a lot more than drink. I'd just give up. There's no way I can imagine getting through that without any support. Looking back at it now, I don't even know how he held it together as much as he did, and that goes for my mom, too. I can look back and wish it was different, and I'm not going to pretend my environment didn't have anything to do with the way I turned out and the mistakes I ended up making. Some of that was stuff I learned that I shouldn't have learned. But I'll tell you what: this family is strong. I'm strong, my brother's strong, and my mom and dad are strong people. They held it together for us the best they could.

Now that I'm an adult who's made my own mistakes, I understand the damage a person's demons can do to the things that matter in their life. I didn't have perfect parents, but you'll see that in the end we did make it back to being a family. I consider myself lucky to be part of a family that's strong enough to survive what we've survived. We're all living proof that it's never too late to make things better.

That said, it still sucked to live through all those shitty parts. There wasn't anything normal about my childhood as far as I'm concerned. And it wasn't just all the chaos and the fighting. We didn't even have a phone when I was growing up! We had one for a little while, but it wasn't working for long, and the worst thing was the actual phone just stayed on the wall in the kitchen forever, like it was mocking us. Eventually, we didn't have TV, either. Some people would say that's a good thing, I know, but for me it was just one less normal thing in my life and one more reason to feel really alone. I didn't get to have that normal kid life where you watch TV and call up your friends to talk and get in trouble for staying up too late on the phone.

There were still a few things I held onto back then. For one thing, my brother and I were best friends. We shared a room all the way up until we started turning into teenagers. We talked every night, and I used to sing to him until we fell asleep. We talked about everything and did everything together. Up until we started getting older and doing our own teenage things, our connection was flawless. And even after our relationship with our dad had fallen apart, Bubby and me totally inherited his love of music. In fact, it turned into one of the most important things in my life. Whatever I was going through, music was the closest thing I ever found to an escape.

I had friends in school, too. I was a goofy kid. I was shy and timid when I didn't know you, but once I did I loved to laugh and joke around. But it's hard living a life where all you hear at home is fighting and violence, and it takes a toll on you. I started to feel so alone. I knew my parents' relationship wasn't normal, and my house wasn't normal. I wouldn't even tell my friends about it, but it seemed like nobody else at school was living that life. Nobody had crazy parents like that.

But even that stuff doesn't really explain how I felt inside. The fact was, in my case, there was even more going on under the surface that spelled trouble. I just always felt alone and out of place, no matter who was with me or how much fun it seemed like I was having. It was like that dark feeling wasn't even connected to what was going on around me, and it just stayed where it was, out of reach but always hanging over me. Even back then I knew it was something that was my own personal problem, this issue I had of just always feeling wrong. People did notice there was something unusual about me, although they didn't usually interpret it in a negative way. I got called an old soul all the time, probably partly because I had to grow up really fast dealing with all that family stuff at a young age. But I didn't feel wise or like I had my shit together because of it. I just felt alone.

♦

I don't remember exactly when someone first told me I had depression, but I was young. It's not until after you grow up and learn about those things that you can look back and think, "Wow, that really wasn't a normal way for a little kid to feel." There was just this dark, empty, lonely feeling inside of me all the time as a kid. I felt like I was miles away from everybody else and always would be. And that's mostly what I remember from the blur of my childhood. That deep, weird loneliness and sadness that you can't really explain away with anything, not even family problems.

I just felt wrong. And all I ever wanted was to *not* feel that way. Instead of a little kid's thoughts, what I had was this constant, painful wish to just feel any other way than the way I felt. All I wanted was to feel different. I wanted to feel normal.

But I was so young, I didn't know what to do. I couldn't change what was going on around me, and I couldn't control that sadness inside of me, either. It was really bad. It was so bad, honestly, that when I was eleven I made the first of many extreme attempts to fix it.

I tried to kill myself.

I can't even explain how I could be so young and decide the right thing to do was end my own life. I don't even know if I wanted to die, exactly. I think I was just in such a haze and feeling so bad inside with that loneliness and confusion, it just seemed like the thing to do, because then I wouldn't feel like that anymore. It's a twisted thing for a kid to think, but with that kind of depression and at such a young age, I guess it was just the only solution I came up with.

No one was home when I did it. I just took a cord into the bathroom and hung it on the fan in the ceiling, and I looped it around my neck. I didn't get on a chair, take a deep breath and jump, or anything dramatic like that. I just leaned into it and picked up my feet. It's so hazy that I only remember certain details, like feeling tons of pressure behind my ears and then waking up on the floor. I don't know how long I was out. But the fan had only been held up in the ceiling with one screw in the middle, and the weight pulled the fan so it stripped the screw and fell on the floor. I didn't try again—I just kind of chalked it up to a failure. And I couldn't get the fan back up right because the screw was stripped, so after that it was always kind of messed up and made this weird sound when it was on. Nobody knew the reason but me, so it was this kind of a spooky reminder of something only I understood. For the rest of the years we lived in that house, I'd notice the messed up sound of that fan and have to remember what I'd done that day.

It almost seems unreal looking back on that, and the way I tell the story even I can understand how weird it is. I've never been good at expressing the emotions I really feel behind things, and it's obvious enough that I don't know the right words to explain how horrific that time was and what I was feeling when I was in that dark place as a kid. I can't explain it. But I am glad I survived, just like I've survived so many other things I've put myself through when I was feeling so messed up inside.

Honestly, that was just the first crazy thing I did to try and knock my head into a different place. Suicide attempt at eleven? That was just the beginning. Before long I'd be trying different strategies, and eventually I'd settle on the pills. I couldn't have seen it coming at the time, but that need I had to kill the bad feelings inside of me and get my mind into a different state was what would lead me down the road to addiction. It would end up taking over my life and almost ruining every chance of happiness I ever had.

All the stupid things like that I've done in my life, any one of them could have really destroyed me. But they haven't. The suicide attempts and drug binges should have killed me, but they didn't. There were many more times to come when I'd wake up and not know how I was still alive. But here I am, stronger than ever, and telling you my story. Maybe it's just dumb luck, but I can't help feeling like someone was watching over me. One thing's for sure, though: after how far I went, I don't take that for granted anymore.

3

Adventures in Anderson

One thing that always seems to surprise people about me is how serious I am about music. And I don't mean I like rock 'n' roll or pop or any one genre. I love *good* music. It doesn't matter what it is. Country, old school, heavy metal . . . if it's good, I'll always want to hear it. I'll even listen to polka if it's damn good polka. I don't care. I'm just serious about music, and I love hearing the best of it. That started back before I was even walking or talking, way back in the days when Bubby and I would take those records of our dad's and play them on our little toy record player. We'd just be rocking out to all those classics, The Beatles and Janis Joplin and the soft rock from the seventies, soaking it up. I loved it all, and I still do.

Even by the time I was in elementary school I was getting into all these different genres. When I was seven, I remember it was all R&B and rap: Boys II Men, Mary J. Blige, Tupac,

Ice Cube. I was really into that stuff. The bubblegum pop on the radio at the time wasn't doing it for me at all. I remember one year my mom tried to get me a Britney Spears CD, and I was absolutely pissed. I hated it! I have to admit, though, I did end up liking the Spice Girls, for some reason. But I think that happened to a lot of people, so, whatever. Sue me.

I was still really into the R&B stuff when I was around thirteen. But it was right around then that Bubby introduced me to my favorite band that ended up staying with me for my whole life. Now, Bubby was a teenager at the time, and I practically worshipped him. Between the two of us, it had always been the kind of thing where whatever he did I had to do it, too. If he dyed his hair, I used the leftover color to dye mine. When he pierced his lip, I went and pierced my lip. We just had the strongest connection. We shared a room right up until we hit puberty, and even after that when we got our own rooms, we'd still stay up late together and talk about everything. So one night he came in with this CD by a band called The Used and put it on. I wasn't into that screamo stuff at the time, so at first I was like, "What is this?" I hated it as a reflex. But he just left it on and fell asleep, and I was lying there on his bed just kind of half-listening when this song "On My Own" came on. If you don't listen to The Used, you might be imagining something different from what this song was. It wasn't the sort of hardcore, screaming shit they were associated with at the time. They're actually a great rock 'n' roll group with a lot of different material, and this was a beautiful, introspective song about loneliness and the struggle of living with it. It really struck a chord with me.

Even though I'd always loved music, for the most part it just made me want to dance and have fun. But this was the first time I had ever experienced a real emotional impact from a song. Of course, you have to remember what was going on at the time. By that time I'd already been living with depression for years, and it was so bad I had already tried to kill myself. So hearing something so beautiful that spoke to those feelings opened up a whole new world to me. From that point on, whenever I felt sad or depressed or alone I turned to music and looked for whatever relief I could find in that emotional connection. It was still the same deal years later in prison, where all you really have to pass the time anyway is your radio and your headphones. I'd be up all night, just like when I was a kid, lying in bed with my headphones on getting lost in that music. The funny thing was everybody in that prison knew how serious that habit was, to the point where even if they had to sanction me, they knew better than to take my headphones away. They knew if they did I would be a total fucking bitch. What can I say? Put me in the corner if you have to, but don't touch the music.

Even now I end the days like that, lying there until three in the morning with my headphones on, always with two hundred songs in my iPhone I can zone out to when I feel like it. My little-kid love of my dad's records turned into a real connection with music and the way it could speak to me, all thanks to some annoying CD of my brother's. So I have to give them both credit for that.

Maybe I should have been a music critic. Who knows? Anyway, I got caught up in a little more than music as I headed into my teenage years.

♦

There are about fifty-six thousand people in Anderson. It's one of those towns where it feels really small when you live in it, but it's still big enough to have a pretty substantial dark side. I mean, pretty much every place in the world has ugly parts to it. Show me a village with five-hundred people and I bet there's a pretty good chance it's got its share of illegal activities and shady people you wouldn't want your kids hanging out with.

Sometimes I think the medium-sized places like Anderson might be even worse than really small towns or really big cities. All I mean by that is, towns of that size have their fair share of shady parts, bad neighborhoods, and sketchy people, but those parts aren't big or crazy enough to get a ton of attention like they get in places like New York or Los Angeles. They're kind of easier to overlook and ignore, if that's what you want to do, but they're just as dangerous if you end up falling into them.

Which is surprisingly easy to do, because a place like Anderson is still small enough that there's not a whole hell of a lot in the way of entertainment. Which means young people end up bored out of their minds. Bored to death. I mean, look, it's not like everybody from Anderson ended up starring on *Teen Mom* and going to jail, okay? I'm not talking shit about the place. I'm just saying it's a recipe for disaster when bored kids get too close to the shady side of a town that gives the illusion of safety. And I'm definitely not the only one who knows that from experience.

When I was in middle school, I was hanging out with people I knew from elementary, the same kids I'd grown up with back in my old neighborhood. And everybody in that scene was into drugs. That was just the way it was. I couldn't tell you how it started with them. I mean, nobody's born a druggie. We were all cute little kids drawing horses and rainbows at some point. But you remember middle school, right?

It's right around then that you start to see the first kids fall into stuff they shouldn't be doing.

My friends were the druggies and bad kids, and they were pretty wild. I think the most telling thing about it is that they all hung out with older people. Every last one of them. When the girls dated, they always dated older guys, and not just a couple of years older, but guys well into their twenties, sometimes closer to thirty. So right off the bat that's not a good crowd you're dealing with. People who are that much older shouldn't be partying with kids who are thirteen, fourteen, fifteen. It's just not a normal thing to do, and nine times out of ten those people come with trouble.

The other big issue was that we were unsupervised all the freakin' time. Between everybody in the group, there was always a house to go to where there was either no adult around, or the adult who was around didn't care. I don't remember it ever being hard to find a place where we weren't going to be supervised. We had a lot of freedom. Or we were just so good at getting it we made it look easy. Either way, my friends were the type that were having sex early, drinking early, doing drugs early. They'd bring pills to school and come to class high, meet up with their older friends afterward, and get rides out to parties they were way too young to be at. And of course I was right there with them. The funny thing is though, as crazy as it sounds considering my reputation these days, back then I was the sober one.

Let that soak in for a minute, right?

But I'm actually serious. Back in those days I was kind of a little goody-goody. I was so against all of the drinking and drugs, and I had very good reasons for feeling that way. Coming from where I was coming from, seeing what addiction had done to my dad and my family life, I didn't want anything to do with alcohol or pot or pills or any of that shit. To a bunch of young kids, it was just fun and partying. But even back then I could see little glimpses of chaos that came with that lifestyle, the violence and the sketchy situations, and I knew it wasn't my scene. Even aside from that, just the idea of being messed up all the time was the absolute last thing I wanted. I didn't want to be like my dad, or even like my mom. I didn't want to be wasted and acting bad. I just wanted things to be good and peaceful in my life.

My brother had the same outlook as me. Both of us were dead set on ending the cycle, staying on the right track, and not repeating any of our parents' mistakes. We used to keep an eye on each other and what was going on, and neither one of us liked to see the other doing anything remotely approaching the party life. Of course we loosened up a bit as we got older. Some of us loosened up a little too much, obviously. But even when we did start experimenting with standard teenager party stuff, we didn't like to hear about each other doing it. It bothered me to think of my brother flirting with things that could lead to addiction, and he felt the same way about me. We just really didn't want to be like that.

So that was the reason I stayed away from that stuff for a long time, even when it was going on literally on all sides of me sometimes. I used to sit around and preach to my friends, trying to clean them up. And if you wonder why a bunch of druggie kids would put up with me nagging them to stop what they were doing, I'll tell you why, straight up. It was because they really were good people, and they knew where I was coming from. Obviously, the friends I'd known for years had been to my house. They'd spent the night and heard my parents screaming, and they totally understood all the reasons I hated alcohol so much. You'd have to be kind of an idiot not to. They knew I just wanted to keep the peace with everything and keep things all good. They respected how I felt.

But I was still an impressionable kid, and obviously when it came right down to it, they didn't think they were doing anything really terrible or wrong. They were just being wild and having fun. Now, I'm not going to sit here and call it typical kid stuff, because you better believe if Leah is out running around in strangers' houses popping pills at age twelve it will be over my dead body. But it wasn't like they were shooting up under bridges or anything. The way I see it, they were goodhearted kids who got mixed up in stuff they shouldn't have been mixed up in, because that's what their childhood friends started doing, and because nobody was watching them close enough to catch on and step in to stop it. And honestly, I didn't even think about that deeply at the time. Even if I didn't like what they were doing, they were my friends and that was how they were having fun with each other all around me. After awhile of me sitting there being the odd one out, my resistance started to fade away. And they still always offered me whatever they were doing, which in that kind of group is really just the polite thing to do.

After awhile I was so used to being around that stuff and having weed or pills offered to me every day, eventually it started creeping in on me. I had already tried weed when I was all of nine years old, thanks to an older friend and her friend who was even older than her. That's the kind of thing I'm talking about. How does a nine-year-old kid end up in that kind of situation? If I had to explain it, I'd say it was always that combination of friends of friends plus no supervision. This world of ours was going on right under everybody's noses, and it was so easy to get away with it we barely even thought about getting caught. At the same time, as my friends got older and more experienced with what they were doing, they had more and more to offer me. By the time I was thirteen, I was getting offered pills almost every day at school. I'd say no, and I'd say no again, and I'd keep saying no. But one day, for some unknown reason, I finally said okay.

Adderall was the first pill I ever took. You probably know what Adderall is, but just in case, it's a really common prescription for people with attention deficit disorders. But it's a stimulant, so like every other stimulant, it gets abused by people who don't need it. Some college students do it to stay up late to study, and some people I knew would just take it to party around the clock. It's easy to abuse.

The person who gave that Adderall to me was a close friend of mine, this beautiful girl with a body and an attitude that were way older than they probably should have been at that age. She and I were together all the time, and she was always dating these older guys who gave her this stuff. Again, the same pattern. That night we were at a laundromat when she pulled these pills out and told me it would be fun. I guess I was bored enough to try them out.

I don't know how many milligrams were in each pill, but I took two of them. It took awhile to kick in, and I didn't know what to expect. I had never taken anything before. After forty minutes I was still shrugging my shoulders and saying "This isn't even working." She just kept telling me to give it a minute. We ended up heading over to my house, where she was going to stay the night. That's when those things suddenly kicked in.

I was freaking out. I remember standing in the living room ranting a mile a minute at my mom, demanding to drive her car. I was pacing around, running in and out of the place, and talking ridiculously fast. It was so bad. My friend wasn't much better off. We got so hung up on driving this car we started talking about stealing it. It was so bad! We stayed up late into the morning, babbling and scheming ways to get away with stealing my mom's car. We didn't actually do anything, but damn that was terrible. Afterward I wasn't really sold on the experience. Of course, in a way it was sort of fun to experience a different kind of feeling, especially since I'd never really been affected by something like that before. But basically it was too much for me.

At the same time, though, you could say the seal had been broken. Adderall wouldn't be the last pill I'd swallow. Not by a long shot. What I didn't realize yet was that there were a lot of different kinds of drugs out there to take, and it would only take me a couple more tries to find something I actually did like. There was even a feeling of false safety that came with that first experience, because once the Adderall had worn off I didn't feel tempted at all to do it again. That kind of reinforced the idea that pills were just something you took for fun, and they lasted a little while and then they were over. But we all know that's a dangerous outlook, and it was the bigger and badder pills that ended up hooking me. It was those opiates. Hydros, Oxy . . .

It's hard to think about it and talk about it in depth now, having been to prison. It's hard to remember what a grip they had on me. Thinking about it gives me a fear of the life they led me into and the person I became when I was on them. And I have every reason to be nervous about that, because from the time I got my very first taste of opiates, the pull they had on me was incredibly strong.

I just loved the way they made me feel. And remember, all I had ever wanted was to feel different. I didn't want to be depressed all the time, feeling alone, feeling like I might as well be dead. And there was other stuff piling onto it back then, too. Turning into a teenager is hard on anybody's self-esteem. I didn't feel pretty or special or smart, and I didn't feel confident around other people. So when I took these pills, it was amazing to me that I could become like a whole other person. I was outgoing. I was friendly. I was talkative. I was hanging out with people without a care in the world. When I was on opiates I became this fun, crazy, "anything goes" kind of person, and I loved it because that was how I had always wanted to be but never could.

Looking back on that, I get incredibly frustrated by how obvious it was that part of the reason I got wrapped up in drugs was that they made me feel like I was fixing some of those depressed feelings I'd had since I was a kid. All I wanted was to feel better, and the pills were the first thing that did that for me. I fell in love with them. I just didn't have the maturity to really grasp what a love affair like that really means. I almost did. I almost sidestepped all that shit when I was so determined to stay clean and sober and live my life right. But as we all know, *almost* doesn't count.

Still, I have to go a little easier on myself at that time. Looking back on it with the knowledge of what those pills did to me years down the line, it's easier to see the signs. But I wasn't an addict yet back in those days. Just a typical dumb kid. And even though it's completely appalling to think that I was doing stuff like that when I was so young, or that any of us were, the fact was I was still pretty straight compared to the people around me. I was never a pothead—weed just didn't really do it for me. And I never drank alcohol. I literally had a hate for alcohol because of my dad. Everything else was game, though. And with all the older people who were always hovering around my friends, there was no shortage of options. Influences like that make a huge difference in how you spend your teenage years. We obviously weren't thinking of these older people as deadbeats, or even questioning why they wanted to hang out with a bunch of junior high school kids. Why would we? Hanging out with older people is one of the coolest things you can do when you're at that age. And to take it a step further, you're almost always gonna jump on whatever chance you get to imitate their behavior. I was no different. I don't consider myself an impressionable person now, but I definitely was at that age. Eventually, it got to where if some kid I thought was cool wanted to share drugs, "No" wasn't my automatic answer anymore.

Even if I wasn't going crazy yet, the scene was getting crazier around me. The stuff we were doing at age thirteen is insane. We were partying like we were in our twenties! Actually, you know what? I know for a fact we were partying a lot harder than a lot of people do at any point in their lives. And I'm not bragging when I say that, either. We were just going way too hard, and we were too immature to see the dangers or the consequences of the things we started getting into. We'd be over at these houses where the parents didn't care at all, no matter who started coming over or how many people. And of course, drugs and alcohol never come without drama. There was a lot of fighting all the time, both girls and guys, people getting wasted and beating up on each other over whatever the hell pissed them off that night. And I hated that in the beginning, just like I hated the drugs and drinking. I was determined to stay out of any violence. But I fell into that stuff, too, and I ended up fighting, too. I even ended up liking it. As much as I tried to resist it, it just got to me.

It's pretty depressing to think about how set I was on acting right, and how I failed at it anyway. But at least I was still a good girl as far as sex was concerned. None of that stuff was happening at all. Of course I thought about it as much as any normal teenager, but I didn't really want to do anything with it. I was scared! The girls around me were way ahead of me on that front, for better or worse. These girls were always dating older guys, and there were always more dudes hanging around. I'd get crushes on them, and sometimes you could tell one of them kind of liked me. But they'd always end up going for one of my friends in the end, because my friends were crazy beautiful girls with amazing, womanly bodies, and I was just kind of timid and chubby. That was a pattern I was used to. I definitely wasn't projecting confidence. I'd been feeling unhappy with my body forever, and I had such low self-esteem I didn't even try to make anything happen. I didn't think anyone would wanna be with me anyways.

◆

In retrospect it's pretty obvious what kind of path I was on. And the transition from middle to high school caused everything to get a lot crazier.

Big things happened when I was around thirteen and fourteen. The biggest thing was that right when I was starting to mess around with trouble, my parents finally got divorced. It was a long time coming, something I'd been hoping for since I was in kindergarten. It's not like I celebrated when it happened or anything, but after all those years of being driven crazy by their screaming and fighting, there was definitely a huge relief that came with the change.

My mom moved out of the house with my brother and me, and we moved into an apartment right across the street from the high school. The change was huge. With my parents no longer living in the same house, it was like the volume finally got turned down and I finally had the peace I wanted. No more having to listen to all that screaming and fighting every night, no more having to deal with my dad being drunk and fighting with everyone. Oh, not to mention the fact that for the first time in my life, I had a home phone. I thought that was pretty much the most exciting thing ever.

But there were a whole lot of negative things that crept in with the change, too. Some of them I could see right away, and some of them I wouldn't understand until later. The first and most obvious thing was that my brother was already going off on his own.

By the time my mom finally packed up and left my dad, Bubby had already gotten so sick and tired of the screaming and fighting we grew up with that he was prepared to leave the first chance he got. One day when he was sixteen, he just packed up his stuff and left to move in with a friend. None of us was really shocked by it. Who could have been? It was probably a peaceful and happy moment for him, getting out of there. I don't remember him saying much of anything or making it a big deal. It was a big deal to me, though. When he moved out after everything we'd been through, I felt like a part of me was gone. It was one of the few good things I'd been able to count on so far. All my life I'd had him there in the house to talk to about whatever was going on. Every time something happened, he and I would hang out and hash it out. Now I'd be in the house alone, and I wouldn't have him there to listen to music and talk with. Almost instantly, I felt even more alone than I already did. I was so pissed at him for leaving me! I was so mad I didn't even go and see him at his place. I don't even think he realized it. He was off being a teenage boy, and I don't blame him one bit for it now. I would have done the same thing if I'd been sixteen at the time. I knew exactly why he went off on his own, and so did my mom and dad. Why would anyone stay in a situation like that if he didn't have to? And for all I know, leaving that house was just something he had to do to keep his head on straight and stay on the right track. When a situation isn't good for you anymore, sometimes you have to go against the grain and do something drastic to escape it. I definitely know what that feels like, and I can easily accept that being the case for him.

Aside from Shawn moving out, there was another drastic change in my life that came along with the divorce and the move. Suddenly, I found myself with a ton of freedom.

My mom has worked constantly for my whole life, which meant I never really saw her as often as some kids see their parents. But after she got divorced from my dad, she got herself a new boyfriend. From that point on, when she wasn't working, she was hanging out with him. So with my brother moved out, my dad out of the picture, and my mom barely around, I suddenly had a house (and a phone!) all to myself. That was freedom on a level I had never even imagined. There was nobody around to see what I might be getting into. And the final part of that perfect storm was that our new house was right across the street from the high school, which made it a convenient headquarters for all my friends and I when we started skipping school and getting into more trouble.

The divorce and the new house made for a fresh start, definitely, but the direction I took off in wasn't really ideal. It was just a lot of freedom all at once. When you go from feeling buried in all this chaos and stupid shit, never having room to breathe, and then all of a sudden there's nobody there and you can do whatever you want . . . well, I guess I ran with it. All that quiet time alone didn't get spent on homework, I'll tell you that much. Instead of focusing on doing good in high school, I ended up going the other way and skipping class to hang out with friends.

I still had the same tight circle of friends who moved from middle to high school with me, and we started getting into trouble right off the bat freshman year. I started skipping on literally the second day of high school. A group of friends and I just walked out of there without a care in the world. It was completely ridiculous, and it was the first of many, many days bailing on class just to hang out and do whatever. That day we ended up wandering down to the nearest gas station, just killing time. There was an older girl in the parking lot, standing by her car, and we all went up and started talking to her. I think she thought we were jumping her at first, this gang of high school freshmen skipping class, coming up and being like, "Nice car!" But we just asked her to take us for a ride.

She wound up taking us to the mall, which is where I found out I was amazing at lying. This cop came up and asked why we weren't in school, and off the top of my head I managed to spin some crazy, elaborate story explaining why we were at the mall. I can't even remember all of what I said—something about me being in alternative school and somebody being in college, maybe—but I remember he bought it. Hook, line, and sinker.

It's crazy to think about how in such a short time I went from being the good girl to suddenly walking out of school and lying to a cop in the same day. Talk about a turning point, huh?

The problem that showed up pretty fast was I was never afraid of getting caught. That's what usually keeps normal kids somewhat in check, right? They're afraid they'll get caught and they'll get grounded or whatever. But I was never afraid of that at all. As a matter of fact, it always felt like I got away with everything. That day was just the first of many examples to come. From that point on, I skipped school all the time. I'd literally go to school just to pick up some friends and walk with them back over to my house. Seriously, I barely even remember being in class half as much as I remember skipping it, although I must have shown up sometimes. The thing is, I don't really remember ever getting in major trouble for that stuff, either. The school would call my mom with some automated message telling her I hadn't been in school that day, but it wasn't like she was home to hear it. I'd get the message while I was hanging out there with my friends and just delete it before she got home. They might want to rethink that system. Just a thought.

I kept breezing by the authorities, too. I can remember being fifteen and running into a plainclothes cop who tried to ask my friends and me what we were up to. I looked him in the eye and asked, "Who the fuck are you?" He showed me his badge. I was like, "Oh." So I had to go back to school that day, but it didn't really stop anything. We were ridiculous. We'd take three lunch periods in a row, walk out of the building in plain sight with teachers yelling at us to come back. It was stupid, the stuff we got away with it. But we kept getting away with it. And like we were going to sit there being bored in class when we knew we could just peace out for the day anytime we wanted! That definitely went to our heads quick.

Obviously, my grades sucked. It was all Ds and Fs. I even failed PE, which is easier to do than it sounds, at least if you put your mind to it like I did. Honestly, the secret is just to sit there and not do anything. The teacher would try and get me to participate in the class, and I'd just be like, "Nah." It wasn't even PEs fault. PE is fine. I just didn't feel like dealing with it.

I was better in history. I loved history. I took the AP class and got way into all the crazy stories and conspiracies, learning about all the wars and the Holocaust, and getting a big crush on John F. Kennedy. I still love JFK! I gave the creative stuff some attention, too. I was a model student in choir, and in art class. I've always drifted toward creative stuff, especially drawing. All through school, my art teachers loved the enthusiasm I put into everything in their classes. They saw a different side of me than my math and science teachers did, I can tell you for sure.

But even considering those exceptions, let's be real. I was doing what I wanted, and what I mostly wanted was to hang out. I definitely started to embrace the social stuff in high school. Since my brother was a senior, I knew pretty much everybody from every grade and they all knew me. Before long I was part of the scene with the skateboarders and the hardcore kids; I had my lip pierced and my nose pierced, and I was all about those skater guys. I finally wound up getting a boyfriend, a cute skateboarder who was really good at guitar. How do you say no? I stayed with that dude for eight months, and come to think of it, we actually had a really good time. It was probably one of my best relationships, if we're allowed to count ninth grade. I think I should be allowed. He ended up breaking up with me, though, because he was wanting to hang out with friends and get high and stuff, and at the time I still wasn't really into it all that much. I was tagging along and dipping in, taking pills here and there, but I couldn't keep up with the people who had thrown themselves into partying. I still wasn't totally sold on the lifestyle.

It was lurking on the edges, though. My brother had already given me trouble about the things I was doing at that point. That's the thing about having a cool older brother in school with you. Everything gets back to them eventually. When Shawn heard I'd been messing around with the pills, he was literally in tears about it. In my mind I was still the good kid in my group, so I didn't automatically see what the big deal was. I wasn't an addict then or doing anything really excessive, I was just fitting in and being a crazy kid. But Bubby was so against it. He wasn't into that stuff at all. Even when he did start partying a little bit, he would never tell me, because he knew I'd hate him for doing it too. It was this weird thing we had where we hated the idea of each other doing drugs. We just had that kind of silent pact not to go down that road. It's not the most typical thing for teenage siblings, I know, but that's how much we cared about each other. When you care about somebody that much, you don't want them doing anything bad, whether or not it's something you're doing yourself. I'm sure that was part of what kept that stuff from blowing up for so long, just having him there to remind me it wasn't what I wanted. I feel bad now that he had that burden of trying to keep me on the straight path. It must have torn him up inside when he realized I was really going down the road we both swore we'd never take.

But that wasn't coming for a while. I hadn't crossed the bridge yet. The fact was, whether or not I was wild at the time, I was still holding back enough to get broken up with for not wanting my boyfriend to party so hard. So I had the skipping going on, and the pills once in awhile, and the crazy friends hanging around my house all the time, but there was some moderation going on.

That lasted for another, oh, ten minutes.

4

Facing the Music

Things got more intense pretty fast. By the time I was fifteen, I was going to the kind of parties I always describe as "the kind of parties you really wouldn't expect a high school girl to go to." That's a nice way of saying they were completely messed up places to be. I mean that in the sense that if any parent found out their daughter was spending time there unsupervised, they'd probably faint and then cry. They just were not your typical teen house parties.

Again, I didn't have one friend who was dating somebody that was our age. I can't stress that enough, because it's a fact that really jumps out at me when I look back and try to understand how everything was so intense for my friends and me in high school. Every girl's boyfriend was in his twenties, and most of them were drug dealers.

I could have kept saying no to those pills for as long as I wanted, but unfortunately I was already setting myself up for situations I shouldn't have really been in. When you're buying drugs, or hanging out with people who do drugs or deal drugs, you eventually get connected to the kind of people you never plan to get connected to. I probably should have tried harder to make friends in history class, or whatever. But what I ended up doing was following the friend-of-a-friend chain to some really dark places.

We were hanging out at houses full of drug dealers and gang bangers. These guys were ten years older than us—one was thirty years old, dating my friend who was in high school with me, a girl who was half his age. He'd come over to the house with a bunch of cocaine and lay it out on the table. That was the kind of ridiculous shit that started popping up. As time went on, we came into contact with more people and more drugs, and it all started to warp our idea of what was okay and what wasn't, assuming we ever had a clear idea to begin with. After that period, I can't even tell you how many drug deals, fights, and guns I've seen. I've seen people get guns pulled on them, people threatening each other and beating each other up over all this awful shit. There was one night when I was out at one of these places with my friends, and they wanted to give us tattoos. I'm glad somebody talked them out of it, but it probably wasn't me. All I remember is lying in a Walmart parking lot that night with my head turned to the side, puking my guts out.

I think of a teenage girl in that kind of situation now and see how shocking it is, that a fifteen or sixteen year old girl would be running around with these twenty-year-old druggies and gang dudes, getting wasted and throwing up in parking lots. Those were dangerous situations. It's obvious to anyone with half a brain. But we were so reckless at the time, we didn't even think about it. Maybe it's just how adaptable we were because of our age, but this insane stuff started feeling normal to us really fast.

Mind you, nobody knew about any of this. My mom was always working or hanging out with her boyfriend. My brother was off doing his thing. And I definitely wasn't on good terms with my dad.

Even after the divorce, I still hated him for the way he was in that house. I wouldn't have even been able to call it mad. I really felt like I despised him, and talking to him or having a relationship with him was pretty much the last thing I expected to do at any point in my life. I was putting a lot of blame on him for my unhappiness as a kid, feeling like it could have been different if he hadn't been drunk and screaming all the time, being mean, calling me names. There was no way to get over the hurt I felt over losing him to his addiction. I had all these memories of being a daddy's girl, and no matter how much pain my family had been through, there was no way to understand how he went from that to being the monster he was when he was drinking and fighting with my mom every night for the rest of my childhood.

So there was no mom and no dad telling me what to do. I was all on my own. And I went all out on the partying. That was all I really wanted to do. It wasn't to the level I'd go to a few years later, not even close. I was just a crazy teenager, basically—nothing too abnormal from what I could tell at the time.

But I was about to get a new influence in my life, somebody who'd wind up having a bigger impact on me than I could possibly imagine at the time. I was about to meet my future fiancé.

◆

He was my brother's friend to start with, but the first time I laid eyes on him was in the school library. My math teacher had sent me there during lunch. I was so behind in my homework, and he strongly suggested I go there and try to get something done. There was a class in there at the time, a senior class, and all of a sudden I saw this guy sitting with his back facing me. He had a football team jersey on, and he was freaking huge. I didn't even see his face, but I remember clearly thinking to myself, "Oh my god, this guy is huge. He's gotta be the biggest guy in the school." He looked like the damn gym teacher.

About a week later, I was sick at home—had a reason to skip, for once—and my brother walked into the house with the guy from the library. He introduced us, and I was thinking, "I just saw that guy a week ago." He was really nice. Really proper and polite. They had just gone and bought this CD, some screamo kind of hardcore metal or something. My brother and me were into that kind of music, but when my brother's friend put it in and listened to it, it was obvious that he wasn't into it at all. He looked at both of us like, "No." Back then he was just this Christian boy straight out of Cicero. He went to church every Sunday—literally, every freaking Sunday. So he left that CD for us. It wasn't his thing.

Some time after that I called the apartment from wherever I was hanging out, and this man picked up the phone. I said, "Hello?" And this guy goes, "I'm layin' in your bed right now."

"Excuse me?" I was freaked. "Who the hell is this?"

"I went through your underwear drawer."

Then I could pretty much hear him grinning. It was totally the Christian guy out of Cicero! He'd gotten into a fight with somebody in his family, and he went and stayed at my mom's house while my brother was at work. He was just playing with me. Never gave me any reason to think he actually went through my underwear drawer. But about a week later, he called the house when I was home and asked if my brother was around. I told him no, he was at work. But then we stayed on the phone. He and I ended up talking for about eight hours that night. What I didn't know was that he had taken my brother to work that night, so he knew he wasn't there. It was a set-up to get me on the phone and ask me on a little date, which he did.

Our first date was amazing. We picked up a couple of friends and went to see *Final Destination*. On the way there I found out there was a lot more to him than meets the eye. He showed up in a nice polo shirt and khaki shorts. Of course I had my lip pierced and my long black hair. I wasn't really sure what to make of him. I was sort of thinking he was some kind of straight-edge football player. But on the way to the movie, his friend Jordan kept saying this weird stuff, going, "Show her your nipples, Dude! Show her your nipples!" The next thing I knew, my movie date lifted up his shirt and showed me that he had his nipples pierced! Not only that, but there was a huge tattoo of a sun in the middle of his chest. I stared at him with my mouth open, like, "What in the hell?" And I remember being relieved, because I had thought he was this goody-goody dude and he definitely was not.

After the movie we all went out and got something to eat, and then we dropped them off and it was just me and my date. We were sitting in the car outside his house and I said, "Oh my god, dude, I can't go home now. I'll get in so much trouble. It's too late." I didn't want to risk going home after my mom had gotten there and having to explain what I was doing. I wanted to act like I'd stayed the night with a friend.

So he said, "Listen, you can just sleep here. I'll stay in the car with you." It was really sweet of him. He was sitting in the driver's seat and I kind of laid on his shoulder. Of course, after about an hour we had to face how uncomfortable it was. So he said, "Hey, maybe I can sneak you inside." We made it into his room and he put his arm out for me to lay on. He was so nervous he was shaking a little bit, his arm was out completely straight. I laid down on it, but I could tell he was freaking out so I started kissing his hand. I kissed all the way up to his arm and all the way to his face and then I started to kiss his lips. I had to give him a little bit of a lesson, but it was really sweet. We just made out that night, nothing else. It was just a perfect night. Then I woke up to him shoving me off the bed onto the floor when his grandpa walked into the room.

Still, even the morning was good. After his grandpa left, he started playing the guitar for me. I love a man with a guitar, but he was very, very good. He's probably the best guitar player I've heard out of any of the guys I've been around. The way he plays is just so gentle, and he has a beautiful singing voice. It's just so pretty. He played a song for me and sang to me a little bit. It was the sweetest thing.

We just had something special. We instantly liked each other and had feelings right from the beginning. To me he was so interesting because he was so different, and he was interested in me for the same reasons. He was the football player, the good Christian boy, playing his guitar all soft; I was the wild child, listening to loud music, partying with these crazy people. But opposites just attract, and we had things in common, too. We both had come from rough childhoods, we were both virgins, we both had jobs and worked really hard, and really wanted to move up from where we'd come from in life.

Honestly, our relationship in the beginning was a fairy tale. It was what everybody wants. We'd sneak out to hang out all night, going to church parking lots and just sitting there for hours, talking and making out. It was so interesting being with him. We would have these really, really long conversations where we would just be staring into each other's eyes, talking about nothing. It was really one of those special things.

There was one night when we were at the movies and he was holding onto my hand, kind of petting it with his thumb, and I felt his grip getting tighter and tighter. When I looked over at him, he had tears in his eyes. I was so surprised I asked him if he was okay and what was wrong. And what he said to me was, "I'm just so happy that I found you."

That was the moment when we both just went, "Okay, this is for real."

We had a few areas where we clashed, of course. As much as I was into him, it wasn't like he was suddenly the only thing going on in my life. I was still blowing off school, and partying was still pretty much at the top of the list of things I wanted to do. He became the only person outside my friends who knew anything about that side of my life, and he did a lot to balance it out. He really tried to get me back into going to class and doing my work, because I was missing so much that I was getting kicked out and sent to alternative school.

He tried to influence me in other ways, too. One huge thing he helped me get over was my eating disorder. I can't even tell you when I started making myself throw up. I know it was very young, and I think I was seven when I realized I was chubbier than some of my friends. I always thought I was ugly, and I always thought I was fat. So I'd been starving myself, overeating, and then making myself throw up since I was in elementary school. He found out about that, and when we got together I was finally able to cut that behavior out and learn to be a little healthier.

I used to tell him when we got together that he saved my life. Sometimes I had a pull on him, too, but we kept each other in check. For example, sometimes he'd skip school just to be around me when I was doing it, and I'd have to be like, "No, you have to go to school." I had no desire to drag him down with any of my bad behavior. But for the most part we had this natural balance that put us both in awe. Each of us knew what the other was thinking, exactly how the other person worked. Our bond was so close and we shared so much together that I really think of my personality as molded around him. And that's not bad, because we had an amazing relationship. When it really comes down to it, I think the most innocent times of my life were the times I spent with him.

But it couldn't go on being perfect like that forever. He probably didn't even know half of the shit I was doing back then, but he hated the pills and the partying. I remember him smacking a bottle of pills out of my hand one time, and another time I remember him finding a different bottle and throwing them out into the road. And that, I could handle. It pissed me off when he wasted my pills, but I wasn't nearly so bad that I couldn't see where he was coming from. I could handle him trying to keep me on the right track, because that was something we did for each other. Unfortunately, what was pushing me away at the same time was how controlling he got. He always wanted to know exactly what I was doing and where I was, or he wanted to be with me every minute of every day. I did, too, at first, but after a while it started to become too much.

It's understandable now how he might have felt. Maybe the reason he was like that was because I'd been partying and pushing him away and stuff, and he didn't want me to leave and go get into some kind of crazy trouble. That would make perfect sense. I couldn't argue. But the way I saw it, I was just a normal crazy teenager, and I was doing what I wanted. At some point, that had become my top priority. I was just doing what I wanted, and that was that. Nobody around me was telling me what normal boundaries were, and so my guiding force was basically that I really didn't like being told what to do. I was so young and so rebellious about it that when I thought of somebody else's disapproval, all I wanted was to go party harder and do more drugs. And he hated it.

We ended up fighting more and more, and eventually we fell into the break-up and make-up cycle. But our relationship had already been established, and there was something so strong and special about our connection that it never really went away. Even when we weren't together, we kept an eye on each other. If he got wind of me being depressed, he'd come right over and try to patch me up. If he called me to see what was up and heard that I was crying, he'd be there in five minutes. It didn't matter what he was doing. And I still loved him, too. I always went back to him. There was one night when he was at his mom's, and for some reason the electricity had been turned off. I was out partying at about three in the morning when somebody told me about it, and immediately the thought of it just took over my mind. I couldn't stop thinking about him and worrying about what that felt like for him, lying at home all alone with the power shut off. That's not a nice situation to be in, and I couldn't stand the thought of him dealing with it all alone. So I bailed on the party I was at and went over to spend the night at his house, just to show him I was there for him and that he didn't have to be alone.

The simple fact is there was never a time back then when I didn't care about him, or even a time when I didn't want to be with him. I was just young and stupid, and I wasn't thinking about a relationship full time. He was older than me, and he was ready for more than I was. I wasn't on his level yet. I had only just started coming into my own and being a rebellious teenager. I just wanted to do what I wanted, go out and party as much as I wanted, and take all the fun I could get. In my mind, I'd gone long enough without it, and it was time to soak it up.

But honestly, things were starting to get darker in my world. While all of that breaking up and making up was going on, there's no question I was moving steadily deeper into a lifestyle I had no hope of keeping control over. Whether I realized it or not, I was starting to figure out how those pills could help me escape the things I didn't know how to deal with, or didn't want to deal with. You can't blame the guy in my life for sensing it was bad news. In the end, he was right to try and get me away from drugs as soon as he could. It's too bad it didn't work.

He wasn't the only man in my life who knew how terrible the consequences of addiction could be. While I was casually popping those pills and brushing off his warnings, my dad was coming face to face with the physical effects of a lifetime of alcoholism. And when that happened, I found myself dealing with one of the most difficult and painful things I had ever experienced.

◆

It's hard to tell the real story of a relationship when it's been through as much as mine has with my dad. I can't ever really explain those years of loving him and then hating him. The ups and downs make it impossible. And back when I was a teenager, I couldn't even make sense of it. That was why I didn't have a relationship with him anymore by the time I was fifteen. I couldn't forget how much I loved him when I was little, and I couldn't forget how much I hated him when I was older for the way he treated the family. I didn't know what to do with that combination.

When it comes to family problems like that, though, you never get to sort through things in your own time. They always end up exploding in your face when you least expect it, forcing you to face things you don't feel ready to face. I had already built up a lot of walls so I wouldn't have to deal with my relationship with my father, and it all came crashing down on me much sooner than I was prepared for.

My dad had been staying at our place for a couple of nights. He'd gotten sick, puking up blood, and his stomach was swelling up really bad. He was having trouble breathing. But after a couple of days he went back home to rest at his own place. That night my mom had a dream that something bad was going to happen to him. It freaked her out so bad that she got up early in the morning and went straight to his house to take him to the hospital.

She was right to trust her instincts. It turned out the fluid in his stomach was squeezing his heart. They drained two freaking liters of fluid from his stomach. If my mom hadn't taken him to the hospital, he would have died in hours.

My dad had been an alcoholic for my entire life. In fact, he was an alcoholic right up until the moment he went to the hospital. That alcoholism had destroyed our relationship.

And it had destroyed his body, too. Now he was in the intensive-care unit with cirrhosis of the liver, and the doctor was giving him eight months to live.

When my brother and I found out, I remember Bubby freaking. He locked himself in the bathroom, yelling and screaming. I was weirdly calm. I remember saying to him, "Quit freaking out. You're gonna be fine." I didn't even think about it. Then I got to the hospital. As soon as I walked in there I started bawling my eyes out so bad I couldn't even make my way into the fucking room. I shocked myself with my own reaction, because I had hated him for so long. But knowing he was in the ICU just got underneath that grudge I was holding and shook a lot of feelings loose.

When my father got out of ICU, he was sober. And that was the craziest shit. He was like a completely different person. He would come over to sit with me and try to talk to me. At that point the shock of seeing him sick had worn off, and I was feeling even more confused and lost than I was before. I just didn't know where to go from there. At that point I still hated him because I couldn't even process this new person that he was. I couldn't remember knowing him sober, outside of those little-kid memories from way back when. But after so many years with my father the alcoholic, they seemed more like dreams than reality. Now that he was sober, it was truly like talking to a stranger. I used to explain it by telling people that the first time I met my dad was when I was sixteen. That's how it felt to me.

Slowly, I got to know him on those new terms. One thing I realized after my dad became sober was how much we have in common. I'm so much like him that it's insane. We both have the same filthy mouth. We're always trying to get a laugh out of people. We're always thinking about random stuff, starting crazy conversations about unexpected things. There's so much of him in me that I never knew about growing up, because I never got to see it past the alcohol.

Our relationship didn't recover right away, though. I didn't leave that hospital planning father-daughter days. When you have that much hurt and anger between a parent and a child, it's not that easy to fix. As stubborn as I am, I don't know how long I might have gone on hating him if the situation hadn't forced me to accept that things had changed.

It started with a big fight between my mom and me. I was so pissed I was threatening to leave. I was telling her I was moving in with my friend and I wasn't ever coming home, and of course she didn't know what to do about it. She was desperate enough to call up my dad and tell him he should come and get me, and he agreed, saying he would come to pick me up and bring me back to his place.

Of course I said there was no way that was happening, but I still got in the car when he came by to get me. I went to his house with him, and before long the argument was on. We got into a huge fight, really big, the kind of fight where it all comes out. I didn't hold anything back. "I fucking hate you. You ruined my life. You ruined my childhood. You ruined your family." And I don't regret a single one of those words. I don't take it back. He was hell, all those years. Seriously hell.

Of course, I wasn't just mad at him that night. It started with the fight with my mom, and by the time my argument with him came to a head I was so worked up and so dead set on running off on my own that he called the police to come calm me down. They told me I needed to stay with a parent. So I went off on the police, too. "You don't understand," I told them. "He's an alcoholic and I can't stand him. He ruined my life. I can't live with him."

It was the most horrible scene. I'm surprised my dad was able to stand it. After years of messing up, all the consequences of his mistakes were blowing up at him all at once. All he could do was stand there with the cops, pleading with me to listen to him and to give him a chance. I wasn't having any of it. I just wanted to be out, away, gone.

And then, he apologized.

It was the first time my father had ever apologized to me. He had never been that type of person before, but somehow I could hear it in his voice and I could see that he meant it. It was hard to even believe. To hear that coming out of his mouth was so powerful. It got through all the hate and anger I was throwing at him and reached the place inside of me that was still hurting because I missed my dad. That apology meant everything to me.

After that day I stayed with him for a while. It was a one-bedroom apartment, so I slept in a bed in the living room. That was one of the lowest points I ever experienced, actually finding out how sick he was and witnessing it firsthand. I'd never stayed with him before, or spent time with him outside of that visit to the ICU. I didn't know what kind of pain he was in, and I wasn't prepared for it at all.

In the mornings I would hear him in his room, groaning really loud in pain, waiting for his painkillers to kick in. I knew it was really bad when I would walk in there and he would be shaking and holding his stomach, holding his rosary, laying there with his eyes closed and pretty much praying not to die.

One day I heard him making these terrible sounds. He was just so obviously in pain. I went into his room and saw him lying there with his rosary, and he was trying his hardest to say he was fine. He told me to stay in the other room, and he was trying to be quiet so I wouldn't know.

Seeing him suffer like that ripped me up in pieces inside. To see a human being in that much pain and struggling to hide it, was horrific. I couldn't escape how bad his condition was. And finally I couldn't escape the feelings I had about it.

That was when I laid on the bed with him, put my arm around him, and started crying. I told him I loved him and I just hugged him and held him. When I did that and showed I accepted his pain and was there for him, he was finally able to sort of let go and handle it the way he needed to handle it. He stopped fighting to stay quiet and let himself make those sounds of pain, and I just held onto him. It was the first time I'd ever done that, and it was the first time I really accepted him as my dad.

It was painful for me to see that all the pain he'd put me through was coming back to him times ten. Maybe the saddest thing about it is that I had to believe he was dying before we were able to have a relationship. He had to get to that point to be able to introduce himself to me as a sober man. I don't have the anger I used to have toward him anymore. Instead, it makes me so sad that we don't have the chance to spend time together when he's not sick. He's the number one person in my life now other than Leah, but I still get so emotional over the time we lost that I have a hard time even talking to him. I just wish he wasn't sick and we could have that relationship that I always wanted.

But at least it's something. And it's taught me never to give up on forgiveness and making it right. People can hurt each other in the worst ways, and they can destroy their relationships, but no one can ever tell me it's impossible to rebuild. You can always start again. It's never too late, and it's never impossible.

5

Happily Ever After, For A While

Forgiving my father was one of the most important moments in my life. I've learned from that experience in so many ways. Unfortunately, I didn't really get all the lessons I could have gotten from what he went through. I could see, right in front of me, how his addiction had destroyed his life and the lives of the people around him. But somehow I couldn't think of myself as the same as him. I couldn't understand that I was steadily sliding down the same path.

While all that was going on with my dad, I was still dating my future fiancé. I was skipping alternative school, and I was fighting with my mom. I did have a job, at least—that's one thing I can say. I've had a job since I was young enough that they had to pay me under the table.

But I was really starting to love those pills, and while I was living with my dad, I started to dip into his painkillers.

Opiates are very serious pills to start out on. Those things are insane. But that's what I was taking as a teenager. Opiates just made me feel happy. It wasn't about relaxing or passing out. They just filled me with happiness and washed away all my problems. It just felt like they kept giving me exactly what I wanted. I wasn't an addict, but I was starting to get there.

It could have gone a lot farther a lot faster if not for one little thing that came up. I think you already know.

I was seventeen and I was back together with my future fiancé. We'd been together off and on for almost three years. I was working at Wendy's and doing pretty awesome. I worked my ass off at that job. I was all set to be promoted to a management position when I turned eighteen, and for me that was great. But then I started feeling really sick all the time.

Of course, what do friends do when you're feeling sick, or having any symptom at all, really? They bring you a pregnancy test. My friend brought mine to me at work. I took it into the bathroom and did what I had to do.

In the next couple of moments, a few things happened. First I said "Oh my god." Then I started bawling my eyes out. Then I walked out the back door, got in my car, and went straight home.

I called my boyfriend up right away. I was crying so hard I could barely speak at first. And of course he always knew something was wrong if I was crying, so right away he got really serious and concerned. "What's wrong? What's happening? Is your brother okay?"

My brother had joined the military and was stationed overseas at the time, and that was the only reason he could think of for why I'd be calling him on the phone in hysterics. Fortunately, he was way off.

"No," I said. "I'm pregnant."

"Oh my god." He sounded completely relieved. "I thought something happened to your brother!"

The way he said it almost made me stop crying for a second. Not because it made me feel better, but because his reaction confused me. I hadn't had time to decide what to expect from his reaction, but I definitely didn't expect him to sound as happy as he did. I was like, what the fuck?

"It's okay," he said. "We're gonna get through this. It's gonna be okay."

He came over to my house, and we didn't waste much time breaking the news to my parents. I called up my mom to have her come over so I could tell her what was up. I think it was actually her birthday the day I found out. She came home for five minutes, which was long enough to sit down, hear the news, freak out a little bit, call my dad, and leave with her boyfriend. Pretty smooth. Can't say I blame her.

With my dad it was a different story. It seemed kind of ironic, actually, that my father made it back into my life just in time for me to get pregnant at seventeen.

"I'm pregnant." Those aren't words any dad wants to hear coming out of his seventeen-year-old daughter, and my father definitely wasn't ready for it. I'll never forget his reaction. He was so pissed he just slowly turned away and went into the kitchen to get away from us for a minute. He was freaking out, and it was obvious he wanted to beat the shit out of my boyfriend. And of course my guy went and said something like, "Don't worry, Shawn, I'm gonna take care of her." Something stupid like that. It did not help. My dad was absolutely furious.

Both of my parents were seriously shocked. They thought I was a virgin. My bad.

I have to say, though, it's almost amazing they didn't see it coming, or something similar. You could say that I was really good at hiding shit. But you could also be honest and ask, "If you're not around, how the hell are you gonna know?" No one was watching me. I had no rules. I had no reasonable boundaries. I had no consequence. So, there's that. I mean, hey, it's whatever o'clock. Do you know where your kids are? If you have no idea what they're up to half the time, prepare to be shocked when it comes out into the open.

Either way, what was done was done, and I was having myself a baby. While the parents were flipping out, my boyfriend and I actually hopped right on it and got to work. Both of us were naturally hard workers, and we worked our asses off getting ready for the baby. I kept working at Wendy's for as long as I could, and we got our money organized and moved into a townhouse together. He had already started going to classes to become a CNA, and I used to go to the diner with him literally every single night to help him study, just drinking hot tea and quizzing him on his exams. He ended up doing amazing on the test and getting a really good job. That made us really proud.

I was working almost full-time from the moment I found out we had a baby on the way. I did all I could to pick up extra hours, staying late to help the managers whenever I got the chance. I finally had to quit at six months because I got sick with gestational diabetes and I had to be careful. My fiancé was working eighteen-hour shifts three days in a row, and I'd stay up all night cleaning the house and trying to plan and prepare as much as I could. At midnight I'd be on the floor scrubbing the stove, and then I'd go take him lunch at four in the morning. I did everything I could think of to make sure that the pregnancy went okay. I even ate right. I did such a good job on the gestational diabetes diet that I lost five pounds in the beginning! Between the two of us, we really were a force of nature getting ready for the baby. We were a great team.

As for the pills, I didn't touch one speck of anything when I was pregnant. I was actually terrified when I saw that positive test result. The very first thing that went through my mind was whether I'd taken something recently enough, and been pregnant long enough, that I'd done something to hurt the baby. Drugs were banned as soon as I saw those lines show up. Doing drugs while pregnant was completely out of the question. I was horrified by even just the thought of it. And honestly, luckily for me, I still wasn't really much of an addict by the time I got pregnant, so it wasn't a struggle at all to quit. I only say that based on the experiences I had later, when I was *really* an addict and it was *really* the battle from Hell to get off of drugs. But at that time, for the pregnancy, no big deal. Even if I had been more addicted, all I had to think of was the fear of that baby coming out with something wrong with her. The thought of it scared the shit out of me. I didn't want to do anything to harm my child.

The point is, I didn't touch a damn thing during my pregnancy. Didn't smoke, didn't drink, didn't take a pill. And it paid off, because Leah came out healthy, beautiful, and smart as hell.

My parents ended up being really supportive of the pregnancy. After they got over the shock of their daughter not being a virgin, I think they were able to calm down once they saw us moving out into a nice townhouse, getting a van, and working our asses off. When I couldn't work anymore I would clean, clean, and clean. We'd do things like go out to rummage sales looking for cute baby clothes and baby stuff. For not having a whole lot of money, we did the best we could do. And I think we did a really good job. To this day, I've never had a parent pay one bill of mine or hand me money. We did it all ourselves.

I want people to know this: you can do it if you have to. The secret is just that you really have to work your ass off. That's all there is too it. There's no trick or hack or coupon that's going to make it easy. It sucks to find ways to support a family when you don't have money to burn. But you can do it if you have to. Pick up more hours, get overtime, get more work. I remember one time when he came home with nine hundred dollars from all the extra shifts he'd gotten. Back then that was so much money to us it was unbelievable. We were excited to the point that he spread the money on the table and took a picture with his phone. We were just staring at it like, "That's a lot of money." It was the most exciting thing in the world. We were going, "We're gonna go out to eat!"

We used that money to help pay off a bunch of bills and buy a good van. We thought that van was the coolest thing in the world. We were really responsible with the money that came in back then.

Still, people can believe it or not, but we had absolutely no idea the show was going to turn into the huge thing it is today. We literally thought it was one of those one-time things MTV always does, like *True Life*, where we were going to be on TV for a little while and everyone would forget about us afterward. Real people are featured on those MTV specials all the time and don't get famous. We had no way of knowing people were going to jump on it like they did or that it would become this huge phenomenon. It's almost mind-blowing to think of how innocently we were looking at the whole thing.

MTV started the filming in the townhouse. They pretty much filmed us moving in together. It always amazes me to think about how many firsts he and I shared together from those years. We had all of the big firsts together, to be perfectly honest. And when it came to the giant first of having a child together, we just worked so damn hard to do it right. We helped each other with money, organized our finances, did everything we could to be responsible. After growing up with nothing, we were so excited to start out on our own, to be able to actually make money and buy the things we needed and wanted. We did a really good job at it.

During that time I really missed my brother. I wished almost more than anything he could be there with me, but he was stuck in the Middle East with the army. There was nothing to do about that. Still, he stayed in touch with me as much as he could and his support always meant a lot to me.

In fact, even though he was all the way overseas, he found a way to be with me in the delivery room. In the footage of me giving birth on *16 & Pregnant*, if you look close, you can see a phone next to my head the whole time I was going through it. That was actually my brother! He had all of his buddies on the base gathered around while I was in labor. I'll never forget him yelling, "What's going on? Why is she screaming?" He was freaking out! But when Leah finally arrived and the whole room started cheering, he and his buddies were all going crazy and screaming and cheering right along with them. It was the funniest, sweetest thing. Not to mention, as far as ways to be welcomed into the world go, that's patriotic as hell.

There were a lot of people in the delivery room when I had Leah, which I honestly didn't think was weird at all. I was having my first baby! I wanted my family to be there. I didn't mind a bunch of people in the room. I needed all the support I could get.

Even so, they all faded into the background once I had her in my arms. She came out crying, of course, and they cleaned her off and handed her to me so I could cradle her on my chest. I'll never forget that moment. As soon as she was in my arms, she literally stopped crying, opened her eyes, and looked straight up at me.

That was when I just melted. I had never felt love like that in my life. Having that little girl look up at me like that, and knowing she was my baby, was the most amazing moment of my life. I remember just being so overwhelmed in that moment, just blown away by that beautiful connection and how huge my love for her was. When I finally looked up at my dad, he was watching the whole thing. I looked up at him almost in a daze, like, "She stopped crying and looked at me!" I will never, ever forget it.

After we brought her home, things were so good. It was just a happy time. I mean, not that it was ever a perfect situation. It was our first baby, and we were young, so we were dealing with all the stress that came with the circumstances. We were also living together for the first time, suddenly having to deal with each other around the clock.

I was taking care of Leah by myself while her father worked, and that was tough sometimes. But he would always come home and tell me he was proud of me, and it made me feel so good.

When he came back from work, he loved to sneak into the house to watch me taking care of Leah. I had this thing I used to do when she first started sitting up by herself. I'd sit her on the bed and turn some music up, and I'd dance around her and make funny faces. I'd sing and act crazy and talk to her, and I'd pick her up and dance with her all around the room. Her little face would be smiling and laughing. He would hide and watch so he could see those moments, and then he'd walk in with a huge smile on his face and hug me and give me a big kiss.

He used to joke around with me and Leah, too. One time she was sleeping in her crib and I was downstairs with the monitor on, and for some reason he came home early and snuck inside. I heard noises through the monitor, like somebody was walking up there, so I went upstairs. I saw Booboo just sitting on the floor, being all calm. I was like, "Oh my god, how did you get out of the crib?" I started freaking out, thinking she fell out of the crib, but I couldn't figure out how. And she was just chillin' on the floor, not crying or anything, looking up at me and probably wondering what my deal was. When I went to pick her up, her dad popped out of his hiding place and cracked up.

When we were all together in the house, there was a lot of music and laughter and love. I'd sit cross-legged on the bed with Leah on my lap facing me, and I'd sing a little song I wrote for her:

"I like to poopy on Mommy, poopy on Daddy, cry cry cry all the time time time... I sleep and drink my milks!"

Trust me, you have to hear it to get the full effect. I would do it in the funniest voice I possibly could, and it would put the biggest smile on her face. All three of us would just crack up.

He would get out his acoustic guitar, and I'd sit there and hold onto her and help her dance while he played guitar and sang little songs for us. Her eyes would just light up when he was playing—you know, that perfect face babies make when they're surprised and their eyes get all wide with excitement. When she started to crawl, she'd crawl on over and reach for the guitar strings, and he'd stop and let her play with them.

They were really happy times. We had such a beautiful little family started. Sadly, though, the cracks were already starting to show. Those wonderful hours started to feel fewer and farther between as he and I got more and more stressed. When it came down to it, we really didn't know how to handle everything that was going on.

Filming with MTV was no problem for us. We liked the crew we worked with, and the money was nice. But when the show blew up, it brought things with it.

All that attention was the last thing we expected. Leah's dad started getting all of these messages on MySpace, all of these girls talking to him. I don't know how many times I saw messages on his account from girls, risqué pictures from all these randos, and him writing back saying, "Ooh, sexy" and things like that. That shit was the basis for a lot of the fights we started having. Of course I replied to some of the people who messaged me sometimes, too, but never like that. He took it to a completely different level.

It started out slow, but we would end up losing ourselves in the money and that weird kind of fame we had landed in. Leah's dad wound up becoming someone who was far, far away from the person he used to be in my memory. But I got away from myself, too, in my own way, with the pills.

Still, I'll say this until I die, and you can ask any honest person. I have never cheated on that man in my life, and he knows it. No matter what life I was living, I never cheated on him. I was always loyal to our relationship. I wish he could say the same.

6

Falling to Pieces

People always ask me how exciting it was when I realized *16 & Pregnant* was making me famous. Well, let me just remind everybody what kind of "famous" that was. I wish I could quote one of the stories directly, but you'll just have to trust me when I go over some of the things the tabloid writers said about us. Or you can see for yourself. It's all over the Internet. The gossip reporters called us schlubby and fat, made vicious fun of our lifestyle and how much money we had, and mocked our relationship relentlessly. It got meaner and meaner as time went on, to where it really just felt like bullying. I'm not even talking about the many times we were criticized in the media for our behavior or our mistakes. I'm talking about the many stories that served absolutely no other purpose than to call us fat or ugly or stupid.

That side of fame wasn't fun for either of us. It was point-less and cruel, and it took a toll.

It didn't happen all at once, but the first signs of what was to come were bad ones. I instantly knew the reality TV thing was out of control the moment I saw myself on *The Soup*. That was a truly shocking moment for me. Like I said, we never thought *16 & Pregnant* was going to turn us into household names. We just thought it was a funny thing that happened one time, and after we cashed that check we were totally ready to fade off into the MTV archives or whatever. We weren't prepared to reach late-night joke status.

It just so happened that *The Soup* was one of my favorite shows at the time. So one night I was sitting around watching Joel McHale cracking jokes when all of a sudden, boom! I popped up on the screen. I didn't even have time to think about whether this was a good thing or a bad thing. It was obviously a bad thing. They went right into it, showing clips of me eating all of this food and making fun of me.

It was the first time I experienced that kind of negative media attention, and all I can say is it made me feel like shit. Straight up shit.

Back then I didn't know what assholes the media were. Maybe it was all that time I spent without a TV growing up, but I just didn't understand how mean people could be. I didn't understand what reason there was for it.

I'd never felt good about food or my weight, and to see myself on one of my favorite shows being bullied for the way I was eating was absolutely devastating for me. I was sensitive, and those remarks cut deep.

That was the experience that kicked off the fame roller-coaster. There was never anything about it that I can say was fun or positive. You can call me ungrateful, but that's the truth. It wasn't like I was walking out on the red carpet with people cheering for me and throwing me flowers. I was getting splashed on tabloids and shows like *The Soup,* and people were not on my side. They'd made their own opinions based on what they saw on the show, and I guess they felt like they knew the whole story and were right to say whatever they wanted about me. They were always picking on my weight and my looks. It was just the hardest way to learn firsthand how vicious the press can be.

So with all that going on, we weren't really excited by the attention so much as we were shocked. Even when people were coming up to us on the street, it was so unexpected and new for us we didn't even know how to deal with it. We were like, "You want a picture with us? What the fuck?" You have to remember we were just two kids in Indiana who'd grown up poor and sad. To get from where we were coming from to having people follow us around with cameras, asking us to pose with them, it was just beyond our comprehension.

I'm not saying I was never excited, but there really was more shock than anything else. I didn't even know how to deal with it or process it, because of course I'd never had that experience before. I remember doing my very first magazine, *People,* with the rest of the girls. They asked us how it felt to be an overnight celebrity. I remember saying, "I don't feel like a celebrity. What are you talking about? That's crazy." It felt more like I was a target for bullying than anything else. After the way it all started out, with all the mean comments about my looks and my weight, I felt completely self-conscious and miserable. I was just buried in that feeling. It really sucked. There was so much of it happening that pretty soon I kind of just wanted to crawl into a damn hole.

I'd always struggled with anxiety, and that shit didn't help. It's all on record how bad I was starting to feel at that time. The stress just starting eating everything up. He and I were both feeling the strain of things. We just didn't know how to handle how fast and how much our lives had changed. All the messages from girls online were still building up in the background, and our relationship was getting really tense. Along with the cruel comments in the media, it just wasn't a good situation.

It came to a point, which people got to see on the show, by the way, where I ended up going to the doctor and getting a prescription for anxiety medication.

That was where the next phase started. I hadn't messed with pills since I found out I was pregnant with Leah. And for six months after she was born, I stayed sober. But I was already reaching the limit with my unhappiness and stress, and I was almost begging for something to come along and offer me a way to escape. A Klonopin prescription was the obvious step for somebody suffering that much anxiety. But almost right away, I started eating them all up, and that was the beginning of me becoming an addict.

Before *16 & Pregnant* had even wound down, they were talking about doing another season. Leah's dad and I were completely sure we weren't gonna get picked. We were still in the mindset that the show was a one-time thing, and we didn't think we were exciting enough to get picked for the spin-off over anybody else who was on the original show.

I'd just gotten that Klonopin prescription when one of the producers came by to see me and let me know we were going to be doing *Teen Mom*. When she walked in and said "You got picked!" I was so blissed out on my new pills I had to think kind of carefully about how to say "Yayyyy . . . woohoo!"

I can't tell you when people started to catch on to those pills being a problem to me. Nobody ever said anything. I don't now if it was because they were afraid of the confrontation or what. At the time, I just thought I was really slick and really good at getting away with stuff.

The thing about going back for another round of reality TV was that even with all the media backlash, we really were excited for the behind the scenes filming experience. We loved the people we were working with, and we got close to everybody right away. All those crew members and people I freaked out with my hillbilly impression in the beginning, we all ended up becoming really close. On their breaks we'd go out to eat together, just Leah's dad and me and the whole crew at the Olive Garden sitting at a big ass table, eating and laughing and cracking up. That's not really normal on the set of a reality show—when the crew is on break, they usually don't want to see your face. But we were all so chill together we hung out all the time. After we were done filming, the girls would stay for an hour after everybody left just to hang out and talk and laugh about shit.

That's the reason why I have the relationships I have with the people from MTV. It's all based on those moments. We built up a really strong dynamic. There was one time during *Teen Mom* when we were sitting and filming and my cousin Krystal was on her way over. When she came to the door, she was all mad as hell and telling me I needed to get my neighbors away from her. "The hell?" I thought, and went outside. To my surprise I saw my neighbor from straight across the street cussing and yelling at me. She'd started up with Krystal over where she parked, like the street had designated parking or something (it didn't). But this woman obviously wanted trouble. It was seriously just some fifty-year-old lady freaking and calling me a whore, walking out into the road like she was about to do something. I don't even know. Of course all I said back was "Shut your damn mouth up. I'm not messing with you. You're like fifty."

Well, right at that moment, this huge blond girl started wandering up the street, and she was yelling and cussing at me, too! "That's my mom! That's my mom!" I was like, damn, is the whole freaking family here? Welcome to Anderson. So there I was standing on the porch in a black miniskirt with a camera crew, going back and forth with this mom and daughter tag team while they closed in on me, screaming I was a whore and acting like they were about to turn it up. They barged straight onto my property, on a rampage and the daughter started getting in my face. So, you know, I got right back in hers. I remember her trying to talk shit to me, saying, "You think you're fucking cute, don't you?" Well, obviously she was an idiot, because that's a really dumb question to ask a smartass. I was like, "Yeah, I am." Duh.

But the crew all came out and they were telling me to walk away from that whole hot mess, so I went back up onto the porch and went inside.

It's a pretty obvious statement, but not everybody in reality TV has that much support from the crew. When everything's all about the ratings and getting the craziest clips possible, it's definitely not automatic that the people behind the wheel are going to have your best interest in mind all the time. And if you don't respect those people you work with every day, if you treat them bad and don't work on building a good relationship with them, you definitely can't expect them to put their asses on the line to have your back when things get out of control. I was crazy back then. If somebody wanted to fight, I was always ready to fight back. It's only because I was lucky enough to have such good people around me that I didn't get into worse shit than I did. Nobody was egging me on or trying to get the most drama for their buck. I really felt they were concerned for me and tried to keep my interests in mind.

It helps a lot to have that support behind the scenes when on the other side, everybody has decided you're a piece of shit. The media was so awful at that time, and so was the public. It wasn't just the mean stories on TMZ and *E! News* or whatever. There were horrible comments on those stories, and messages I was getting, and cruel things on Twitter . . . just all over the Internet. Let me tell you, Farrah and I might have our differences, but it sucks to see her taking on my old role. I know how that girl feels and then some. It's not right. It's really not. Once people decide to hate on somebody, they are relentless.

It used to hurt me so bad when people said things. Back in the day when I got up to around 175 pounds, every time someone said something about my body it cut me straight to the bone. Anytime someone called me fat or ugly, I really believed it. I got so depressed over it, and then I started losing a lot of weight. It probably went a bit too far. I remember going shopping with Leah's dad and trying on some jeans, because the ones I was wearing weren't fitting right. The next thing I knew I was in the dressing room zipping up a pair of size zero pants. I remember him looking at me like, "What the hell?"

I'd never been that skinny before in my life. It brought some of my confidence back, but there was still a whole lot of mess going on underneath that new look. Obviously fitting into a pair of size zeroes doesn't mean a lot when your family's a mess, you've got a kid at home, and you're slowly jacking up your addiction to pills.

Things weren't right on Leah's father's end, either. It's hard for me to look back and speak for what he was going through at the time. I know how the experience affected me, and I know the kind of feelings I had and how I started slipping out of control. But with him, it's hard for me to say. The best I can explain it is that having all that money and all that attention from girls for the first time in his life just did something to change him. He went from being this beautiful person I'd started a life with to being a guy I didn't recognize anymore. The way he talked to me and treated me was completely different. He was doing these mean little things, saying things to pick at me and start fights when there was no reason to be fighting. And the whole time he was getting all these messages from girls and he was sending them back.

It was actually Valentine's Day when things between me and Leah's father took a turn for the worse. Sounds shitty, huh? Yeah. Just wait.

He said he hadn't had a chance to pick me up anything for Valentine's Day, so he took off to go to the mall and get it together a little late. That was about an hour's drive away, so I didn't think much of it when he didn't come back right away. It took about four hours before I started really wondering, and I called him up to check in and see where he was.

He answered the phone. But when we were talking, I heard the sound of girls laughing in the background. That put me on guard. I asked him what the hell was up.

"I was at the mall," he said. "These two girls recognized me and we got to talking, so I was giving them a ride home."

There was so much that was weird about that, to me, I couldn't even think of what to say except, "Really?" I mean, *really?* The man left me alone at home on Valentine's Day saying he was going to go get me something nice, and the next thing I know he's off hanging out with other girls while I wonder where he is? Who would be okay with that? We started getting into a fight on the phone, and it was a really bad fight. But right then, when I was so upset, he started laughing at me. He was laughing at how mad I was, and that wasn't even the worst thing.

The girls were laughing at me, too. He'd put me on speaker. It was Valentine's Day, he was hanging out with other girls, and he had me on speaker so they could laugh at how upset I was about it. I couldn't believe it. After I hung up, I just sat there feeling so shocked and hurt that I didn't know what to do with myself.

It was about eight at night when he got home, and the trouble continued. Instead of apologizing or talking about what had happened that day, he immediately picked a fight with me over what I was watching on TV. It was just a UFC match or something. I was into that kind of thing for a while back then, training in Krav Maga and all of that. But he walked in and picked a fight with me saying I was only watching UFC so I could check out the guys. He used that as an excuse to get all worked up, and then he left.

I should have known what was going on. It's almost textbook behavior for someone to throw those weird accusations around when in reality they're the one off doing something they're not supposed to do. The way he tried to shift the focus on me, like I was breaking the rules or doing something bad by watching a sport on TV that involved shirtless guys, should have told me he was up to no good. But I wasn't prepared to see it coming. After he flipped out over me watching UFC, he said he was peacing out to go stay with his mom for a few days. But the truth came out fast. Before long, he called me up crying, or at least acting like he was crying, and saying he had something to tell me. You already know what it was, right?

"I cheated on you."

Those weren't girls he just picked up at the mall. He didn't even go to the mall to get me a present for Valentine's Day. He went to hang out with those girls because he was messing around with one of them. The whole time that day he was ignoring me, fighting with me, laughing at me, and insulting me, acting like I was doing something wrong, accusing me of checking out other guys on TV, leaving me alone on Valentine's Day, he was doing it right beside the girl he cheated on me with. And he had her laughing at me.

Nothing between us was ever the same after that. Something just snapped in me that Valentine's Day. It was the straw that broke our back. I look back on that day as the day everything between us completely changed. I never in a million years thought that man would cheat on me. Yeah, things had gotten harder and we weren't happy together like we used to be, but I still had in my mind that beautiful, sweet person who used to break into tears if he thought he'd hurt somebody. The man I knew and fell in love with couldn't stand anybody being mean to somebody. He couldn't stand the thought of hurting somebody. And here he was breaking my heart.

It was hard to let go of what had been between us. Even as much as that incident hurt me and changed the way I could handle the relationship, our bond was still deep, and it was still strong. We'd shared so much together, and of course we still shared Leah. That closeness and that life and love we shared were always the reasons we never stayed broken up, no matter how bad we fought.

But it was different this time. That betrayal just did something to me inside. The cracks had been forming for a long time, and they'd come from a lot of places. But finally they just got to be too much. My family was the only thing that ever held me back from the edge. But when that wall came up between me and Leah's father, it was only a matter of time everything else started falling apart. It did not take long.

Hanging with the family

Back in the day with Bubby

Bubby and Booboo

Whatchu' looking at?

Landyn and Booboo hanging out

Booboo in her early walking days

Booboo's first driving lesson

Just bought a Booboo!

Me and Booboo in front of the Christmas Tree

Booboo did my hair!

Just looking cute . . .

Bubby on the bull

TOP: So proud of my brother and all the troops fighting for us.
BOTTOM: Sad day watching my brother leave for Iraq. So thankful he's back here with me now.

TOP: This girl is so damn loved
BOTTOM: Mom and dad *actually* standing together . . . WHAT?

Looking innocent
with Krystal

Just sitting there looking super happy . . .

Seeing myself on the cover of In Touch

7

Behind the Scenes Destruction

Yeah, I know most of you see where this is headed. If you're reading this book, chances are you know enough about *Teen Mom* to know how one of the lowest points of my life turned into one of the show's most shocking clips. You know, the one of me losing my temper and physically attacking the father of my child.

I didn't write this book to make excuses for my behavior. And I'm not denying anything we all know is true. I'm just telling a part of the story that people don't know. So when I talk about what happened, I don't want anybody doubting how much I regret the things I did to hurt people, or how sorry I am about it. I know I was messed up, my behavior was wrong, and there's no excuse for abusing people in your life. And me, of all people, I should have known better. I *did* know better. I just messed up anyway. I'm not trying to justify it. It's a horrible way to act and that person I was at the time is a person I've worked really hard not to be.

But you can't change the past, as much as you might like to. All you can do is try to look back with a clear mind, see where you went wrong, make amends where you can, and move forward. It's never too late to do that, and I've tried hard to make it happen for myself and for the people around me. Even when it means facing how horrible the reality was when things were going wrong.

Even before he cheated, we were in trouble as a couple. And I mean *trouble*. The fighting was bad. But still, the cheating was just the worst fucking thing. I was so hurt it just crushed me. I never in my life, ever, dreamed that he would *ever* cheat on me. Never in my life did I dream he would do that.

The whole thing was kept under wraps. He actually filmed with this girl one time, and people who were watching didn't realize he'd cheated on me with her. It was kept covered up for a long time. And the twisted thing was that I was part of that cover-up. He was the love of my life and the father of my daughter, and even with all the bullshit blowing up between us, I was still trying to fix our relationship. There was nothing simple or easy about the idea of breaking up with him for good, especially since we'd split up and reunited so many times already in our history. It wasn't just the fact that we'd been together so long and had so much love and so many memories between us. The fact was that we shared a child. We were family. So even as things between us got worse and worse, we did still try to force the pieces back together. At least, I did. I can only speak for myself.

So all through this time, there were things happening behind the scenes that I didn't talk about, because I didn't really want our business out there when I was trying as hard as I could not to give up on my family. Off camera we kept on talking and fighting it out, just looking for any possible way we could hold things together. We tried to work it out about a month after he told me he cheated. He came over to my place one night to see me, and we just had a wonderful time with each other. I made dinner, and we talked and hung out for awhile, and then we put on a movie and fell asleep in each other's arms. It was really nice. It was the kind of night that made me remember what we had in the beginning. It made me remember the love I thought we were still capable of sharing. As I fell asleep with him like that, I was feeling good about us and our chances of fixing what we had.

I woke up around five in the morning and he was gone. The movie was turned off. I was in the dark, alone. And I heard these faint sounds like voices out in my living room. This was my house, let me mention. I paid for it. He wasn't living there anymore.

When I heard someone talking out there, I got up and sort of quietly went down the hallway to listen. And there he was, on the phone, talking to this girl.

In my freaking house, he was sitting there talking to the girl he cheated on me with.

I flipped on the light and I was like, "What the fuck are you doing?" And what he said to me was something like, "Quit it, Amber." Like I was the one acting insane, and like he had no intention of hanging up that phone.

I could not believe my ears. I asked him, "Are you fucking serious right now?"

He held his hand up and said, "Stop it. You're makin' her feel bad." He wouldn't hang up. He was sitting there bitching at me for making this girl feel . . . what? I don't know. I couldn't believe it. And I was so shocked, I didn't even get mad. I walked out into the living room and sat on the couch bawling my eyes out, begging him to hang up the phone. And he wouldn't.

What the hell kind of way to act is that? This is the same man who used to care so much about others it would kill him to hurt somebody like that, and who I still have so much love for in my heart, and is such a big piece of my life. And here he was cheating on me and coming over to my freaking house to act all sweet with me and make me feel good about us, and then he's calling this girl up and telling me to leave him alone. It's crazy how somebody can show such different sides.

I don't know how to explain what happened to him. But I do think, hypothetically speaking, of course, that an experience like a reality show can turn a regular person into a piece of shit. That man was less than a boy at the time. To me, behind closed doors with the cameras off, as far as I could tell, he was nothing but a cheater and a liar. And nobody knew because by that time I was already so used to trying to hold up the routine. And I know people might think they know how bad it was from what they saw, but what was inside our world, what we did keep from showing other people, was even worse.

There were times we'd physically fight, both of us. He'd spit in my face and I'd spit back in his face. He'd hold me down and lay on me, all three-hundred seventy-five pounds, and I'd be fighting and telling him he better knock me out because if I got up I'd beat the hell out of him. That was our lowest point. We hated each other for what we thought we'd done to each other, and we got to just about the worst place in our relationship that you can imagine.

I don't know exactly when it became so bad between us. I can't really pinpoint where it happened for him. I know for me, I checked out when he cheated, and I checked out double when things went bad later, when I lost Leah. But I don't know what happened for him. I can't speak for him. From all I can try to understand, I think it was the attention and the money that did that to him.

Today our relationship is confusing. It's very, very sad. It's one of those tragic situations where two people share so much and have grown so much together that they'd love to be together if it was possible. But they've hurt each other so bad, it's not possible at all. Every time I look at him, all I see is all that heartache and pain, and it's even worse that it's all mixed up in love and family ties. It makes me want to jump out of my skin, because I still get caught up in what he used to be. I always think that one day he's gonna come back and be that beautiful person I could count on, the one who said to me, "We're gonna get through this" and meant it. It just breaks my heart because I know that in a perfect world we would have had an amazing life together. But we're so scared of going back to that low point we went to, we're probably never going to be able to give each other a chance to try again.

Those scenes on *Teen Mom* of me beating up on Leah's dad don't really leave any room for doubt about how completely destroyed we were at that point. How do you come back from that? I was wrong to get violent with him. Even back then, I never would have said behavior like that was okay, especially in a family. I know it was despicable and I take full responsibility. And there's no "but" about that, just the added fact that even if he forgave me for what I did to him, there was a whole lot still left between us that couldn't be forgiven. There was nothing we could think of to repair how bad things had gotten.

And once it was over, when I had given up and truly wasn't with him anymore, I just started going haywire.

By the way, he and I never forgot about Leah. We love our daughter and we would never forget what that meant. Nothing that's happened between us ever stopped us from caring about our daughter and the life we were giving her. We lost control of our relationship with each other, and what we'd had together ended up smashed to pieces, but that didn't mean we ever forgot our child in our home. You have to remember we had come from growing up in messed up homes ourselves, and we knew what it was like to live with parents who were screaming and fighting and getting physical. It's devastating that we let that happen to us as a couple, as a family, and I wish more than anything we hadn't ended up that way. Things were just really hard, and we couldn't handle it. The stress and anxiety and anger and hurt were just filling up that house no matter how hard we tried to fight it back, to the point where I was feeling like I lost my mind.

We weren't holding up the routine anymore, and it's not like this was happening behind closed doors. And all of a sudden, we weren't the only ones worried about our child. When the show aired and everybody saw the footage of me beating up on him, there was a lot more scrutiny coming from all directions on how all this was affecting Leah. Obviously the most important place it came from was Child Protective Services.

After I hit Leah's dad on TV, CPS started a file on us and wound up monitoring us for six months. That put even more pressure on us, because we never wanted to get in trouble with them. To make it even worse, the court picked up the case and they brought battery charges against me. That brought along a no-contact order, which was absolutely devastating.

The no-contact order meant that he and I weren't allowed to be around each other with Leah. We weren't even allowed to call each other on the phone. Now, how was that supposed to work when we had a kid together? We still had our child, and the court pretty much made it impossible to co-parent while they stayed on our asses with their investigation. The restrictions combined with our problems getting along added up to a completely impossible situation.

Then, in another charming twist on my fame experience, my house got vandalized and trashed. Because of that, CPS decided it wasn't safe for Leah to stay with me overnight. So before I even knew it, I lost a lot of control over the time I spent with her. Since she was with her father every morning and every night, I had to count on him or the people around him to communicate with me for everything in between. That didn't always work out so well. As a mom, pretty much the bare minimum you can ask for is the ability to know where your little girl is at any given time. But whether it was on purpose or not, there were many times when my calls went unanswered and there was nothing I could do to see or talk to my daughter.

He and I fought to have the no-contact order removed so that we could handle things better and have a better parenting situation for Leah. The judge finally agreed to modify the arrangement, but there was a huge catch. Even though we could talk and hang out as much as we wanted, Leah wasn't allowed to be present during those times. The idea was they wanted to protect her from the problems between her parents. But what happened was it made it so that the only time the three of us could be together was the few minutes during pick-ups and drop-offs.

Even when things did go as well as possible, it was heart-breaking. Absolutely heartbreaking. When I'd take Leah back to her father after spending time with her, there would be a few moments where she was so happy to see her dad. Then she'd realize I was leaving and she'd just fall apart. There's no way to explain to a child that young why one of her parents was always walking out the door when she came around. When I had to kiss her goodbye and she was on the floor crying and screaming that she needed me, begging me to just wait, not to go, it was the most horrible feeling in the world. No matter what anybody thinks of me as a mom, then and now, Leah and I have always had a deep bond, and that ripped my heart out. I couldn't explain to my daughter why I kept leaving her, why I couldn't be with her. I don't think any mom can go through that and not be affected in the worst way.

Meanwhile depression and anxiety were pulling me down, and I was having a hard time finding happiness in anything. I agreed to work on anger management while the investigation was going on, and I was on a lot of medication to deal with my anxiety attacks and depression. But nothing was making me feel better. I felt like a complete failure, and everybody was telling me I was. Strangers were calling me worthless and saying I didn't deserve to be a mom. People were saying I should kill myself.

It was almost like I started living up to what they were saying without even thinking about it, and at one point I did try once again to take my own life. It was right after I was found guilty of the battery charges and right before I headed to rehab. But we'll get to that in a minute.

♦

In fact, let me stop for a minute and talk about the whens and wheres of my story. This might come as a shock, but being on a bunch of opiates isn't all that great for your memory. Even though I was technically present and aware at the time, when I try to look back now I find a lot of the details missing. What happened, and when, and in what order—damned if I know sometimes. That's just one more problem with doing drugs. You can't remember whether you did some awful thing or another before or after you went to rehab, or how many days or weeks or months went by in between. Things get all fucked up and blurry. Looking back, a lot of times I have to take somebody else's word for it on how things went down.

But I can tell you that the day I signed over custody rights to Leah's father was the day I completely broke. I felt like such a failure. People might have seen me talking about it on camera and they could see I wasn't happy at all. But on the inside it was so much worse than that. It was like getting sucked into a whirlpool. Everything that happened around that time is a complete jumble, because after I lost Leah I literally went insane.

That was the one thing that had been kind of holding me together. I know it's not fair to put this on a kid, but at the time, Leah was the only thing that was keeping me decent. I don't give a shit what everybody had to say about it at the time, about my parenting skills or what they saw of my relationship with my daughter. I loved her with all my heart. When I agreed to sign over custody to Leah's dad, I was trying to do the best thing for her by getting CPS off our backs and making it easier for us to spend time with her together. But it doesn't matter what the circumstances are when it comes to how you feel about giving up parental rights to your child. It was the hardest thing to do in the entire world. Even though I believed him when he said it wasn't going to be used against me to keep me from seeing Leah, every time things got ugly between us I felt so uncertain and scared that I had no right to her as a mom anymore. I had given up my control, and I was the one who signed the papers. But the way I looked at it, it really felt like my daughter had been taken away from me.

It just felt like I was backed into a corner. If things hadn't gotten so bad in the first place, CPS wouldn't have been on our asses the way they were. That damn no-contact order wouldn't have kept my daughter and her father from being around me at the same time. The fact was, signing that custody agreement didn't feel like some kind of empowered choice I made. I did it because the legal situation basically had my family held hostage.

After it sank in that I'd lost my rights as a parent, I literally didn't care anymore. I remember thinking, "There's no point now. I'm not even allowed to be a mom. I might as well get crazy."

It was a bad time. I started going out, fighting, and partying. It spun off so fast I can't even explain it. Until then, I'd kept as much of a grip on my issues as I could because I was focused on Leah and trying to get things back in order for her. But once that was off the table, I finally got to a place where the attention and money started getting to me, too.

I was doing whatever I wanted, and I didn't do anything in moderation. It was always extreme when it came to partying and sex. When it really got down to it, my life at that time was nothing but pills and men. I used to get boyfriends for three months at a time, get bored, leave them, and go find another guy. I never thought there was a problem with it. I mean, serial monogamy is the rule these days. But looking back I think it's obvious I had a bad sex addiction along with the pill addiction. And those lifestyles go hand in hand. They feed each other. I used to get into fights with boyfriends over how much sex I wanted. If they weren't in the mood or they were too tired, I would go off. How insane is that? I don't know what I was trying to satisfy in myself. Probably the same thing I'd always been trying to satisfy, just in a new way. I had a lot of fun—I mean, come on. Obviously. But on the whole, I didn't get much good out of it, and I definitely got some bad. Two of those boyfriends sold stories about me where they said they couldn't keep up with me, and I could be a porn star. You know, just your average gentlemanly behavior.

♦

After I'd gone a little ways down that road, I ended up not giving a shit about Leah's father anymore. Meanwhile, he was yapping in my ear like a Chihuahua. The man would come over and dig through my trash can for condoms, even though we were completely broken up.

Oh, the drama. At the time he was saying that he wasn't having sex with anybody, and he was trying to get back together with me. I was actually considering it. Little did I know he had been sleeping with this other girl for a couple of months.

One day I got a random text from somebody saying she got my number from a friend and wanted to hang out. But then she called me up on the phone, and who did I hear in the background? None other than Leah's father. That seemed to explain where she got my number. When he asked her who she was talking to, she said, "I'm talking to my friend Amanda." So it was pretty obvious something fishy was going on. I don't know what her deal was. I think she just cared about the MTV stuff and wanted to be around us, maybe hoping a camera would show up and she'd get her face on the color TV or something.

Needless to say, I had no interest in hanging out with her, but she kept texting me and stuff. In my mind I knew they were messing around, and when she mentioned they were hanging out, I just knew.

What can I say? I got a little mean. One day when she texted me to hang out I said, "Okay, fine, drive to my house and we'll go out." Now, let me just mention I was looking pretty damn good at the time, and that day I dressed up to the T. White spandex and heels, man. I was at my peak.

When she showed up, we did the small talk bullshit for awhile before I said, "Okay, let's take my car."

But I'd already been scheming. I was talking to Leah's father just an hour before she showed up, and I asked what he was doing that day. He said he was gonna be hanging out at home with his friend Joe. So I pulled out of the driveway and started heading over. When the girl asked where we were going, I just casually said, "Oh, we're going to my old boyfriend's house."

She started freaking out a little bit and asking why we were headed there, but I was just like, "Because that's where we're going." I drove us there, got out of the car, and walked right up to the house. Leah's father opened the door and saw the girl sitting in my car. His face was absolutely priceless. I just said, "What's up?" And I walked into the house.

The girl got up and followed me, and I could see the look in his eyes as he was shaking his head at me like, "What the hell . . . this crazy bitch." That's when I looked at him and said, "Yeah, what's up? So, pick one."

And guess what? He picked me.

Not like that made a difference to me at that point. All I did was turn around and look at the girl like, "That's right, bitch." Let her deal with him, was the only thought I had on the matter. My give-a-fucks were gone.

The poor girl was obviously in over her head. She was just kind of cowering on the side and looking at me like, "Oh my god. My car's at your house..."

So I was a bad bitch for a minute there, and that was satis-fying. Of course, then I realized I had locked my keys in my car. We had to wait for somebody to come and unlock it. That was a little awkward. Then I found out my tags were expired or something when I got pulled over on the way home, with this girl in my car. By the time she finally got behind her own wheel and drove off, I was pretty bored of the whole thing.

Oh, and just to be clear, I did *not* get back together with my ex. As far as any chance of romance was concerned, I had made up my mind and I was done with him.

One thing I know one-hundred percent about myself is I have the ability to make some tough-ass choices when I have to. Deciding to stay away from Leah's father was one of those big decisions I made when I looked around and just had this wake-up moment, and I realized I didn't want to be stuck in that terrible situation.

Like I said, I never really feared consequences as much as a normal person should have, and I was never held back from doing anything by any fear of regretting it later. It's actually the opposite. I have this fear deep down inside of being on my deathbed and thinking, "I wish I would have done that." I don't want to look back and regret what I *didn't* do to save myself because I was letting pain hold me down. I don't want to ruin my life and then sit there looking back and seeing where I missed the chance to get back on track.

When I have that clarity, I have the strength to make those drastic moves. And that's just my style. Not doing anything in moderation can be really bad in a lot of ways, but when you're really feeling stuck in a bad situation, you have to be ready to go to the extreme and say, "Enough is enough." For me, it was a skill that would come in handy later, when I found myself needing an emergency exit once again.

I wasn't there yet, though. In fact I felt like I was in the tiny eye of a horrible storm. Everything around me sucked. Everything had fallen apart. And as far as I could tell, I had nothing to lose. It was not a good state to be in.

8

There's More Than One Way to Rehab

I'm going to share some life advice with you now, just a piece of wisdom earned through my own unique experience. The advice is this: if you have paparazzi knocking on your door saying, "Hey, I heard you're fun to party with," chances are you're doing something wrong with your life. Just make a note of that somewhere.

The media attention I was getting at that point was ridiculous. I'd walk up to my house and there would be four cars just sitting there out in front. Just a bunch of paparazzi in Anderson, Indiana for no damn reason but to follow around the notorious *Teen Mom* Amber Portwood and hope she did something juicy enough to sell a picture of. And, well, to be fair, they were on the right track. I was wild as hell at that point, and doing everything I could think of to go even wilder.

In the last few months, it felt like I'd lost my grip on every good influence that had been keeping me somewhat sane. My family had totally fallen apart, and I couldn't see a shred of hope that it would ever go back to the way it was supposed to be. I'd given up custody of Leah and failed to figure out how to handle co-parenting with her dad. All my expectations and responsibilities were a complete mess.

So what did I do? I turned to partying.

The conditions were right for it to happen. Not only was I feeling completely miserable and desperate for a distraction, but I'd finally gotten to where I didn't care about the mean things people said about my looks or my body, and I had some sense of confidence back. In fact, I guess because of all the stress, I had lost an insane amount of weight after having Leah. After all the bullying I'd experienced for my size, the urge to dress up and go out and show off how awesome I looked was a way to strike back and settle that score in my own mind. When the paparazzi came knocking and asking me to party, they could have been anybody. I was ready to go out and stir some shit up. There was nothing healthy about my mindset at the time. There were definitely much better ways I could have handled the hopelessness and heartbreak I was feeling. But there were also plenty of new faces who were more than eager to egg me on in my mission to go crazy. Yes, including the paparazzi.

I was pretty good at avoiding them, usually. I'd just sneak in and out of my house through the back. But there was one time when I'd just gotten out of the shower and I heard a knock on the door. I went and answered in a towel, and so of course there were four guys standing there. That's how fate works. One of them was a guy from a pretty well-known publication who said he'd heard I could party. He must have heard it from some people I'd gone out with the night before. I don't know. But these guys wanted to hang out, so I went along and partied with them at the hotel where they were staying.

You think teenaged reality TV stars are crazy? Well, listen up: paparazzi are crazy. At least the ones I know. Those guys go hard, and they just live in a really weird kind of world where it's normal to act completely insane. I remember them showing me all the photos they'd taken lately on their computer, pictures of Brad Pitt and the cast of *Twilight*. One of them had a bunch he'd taken while he was hiding in trees in the woods and stuff. There was one guy there I really liked, through. He did a lot of high-end stuff, photo shoots for *Vogue* and everything. Another of them just sold to tabloids and all of that. But the kind of important thing was that they were all pretty damn hot. We went to the hotel and stayed the whole night hanging out and partying. There were people there who were trading pills and getting all messed up. We got crazy in the hot tub, rocking out and acting wild, and early in the morning we went back out and these guys stole a bunch of balloons from some store parking lot and handed them to me. There were pictures online of me walking down the street with this big bunch of balloons while they were just taking photos of me. Weird kind of trade-off, right? We all got to party, I got balloons, they sold their pictures, and the world got to see another wacky *Teen Mom* candid.

We all know it wasn't all fun and games, though. I was pretty much living as fast as I figured out how to do, going out as often I could, and taking pills by the handful. Somehow this was still a secret by the time I went to rehab.

My life was just a roller coaster of extremes at that point. I felt like I was having the time of my life when I was out partying and taking pills, trying to kill off my feelings and remove myself from all my worries. But in the daytime it was usually a different story. The fact that I didn't have my daughter anymore was always hanging over me in the back of my mind. And the consequences of hitting Leah's father hadn't even fully come down on me.

♦

I had been hit with two felony domestic battery charges, along with a charge of felony child neglect that was eventually dropped. The reason the charges were so serious was that people were saying I had beaten up Leah's father in front of Leah, which is a bigger crime than if I had hit him in private. I fought the charges, but they were riding my ass and pretty soon it became clear that I wasn't going to be allowed to walk away from that situation without some kind of serious legal consequence. I was facing three years in jail if I was convicted of that, and my odds just weren't looking good. Finally, I decided to strike a plea deal to stay out of prison. In exchange for my pleading guilty to the battery charges, the judge put me on probation and told me I had to complete thirty days in an inpatient treatment facility to deal with my anger management. He also ordered me to get my high school diploma and to put ten thousand dollars in a college fund for Leah.

It could have been a lot worse, but that was not the way I looked at it. The glass definitely wasn't half-full. The way I saw it, it was empty and cracked on the floor. Being found guilty of those battery charges felt like the nail in the coffin of my sanity. Any work I was going to do in the interest of anger management, I felt like I probably should have done long, long before I lost control and wound up in such a horrible situation. I was already so overwhelmed by stress at the time, between my toxic relationship with my former fiancé, my anxiety and depression, not being able to see Leah, and keeping up the constant juggling act with all the pills I was taking. The way the media and strangers were talking about *Teen Mom* had me feeling like public enemy number one. They were saying I was worthless, that I wasn't fit to be a mom, and the worst of them were that I should just go and kill myself.

On the outside, whether it was on camera or just the way I was acting in front of the people who knew me, I was angry. That was the side that people saw. I had such a short fuse at that point, and I'd never been exactly easygoing to begin with. The more anxiety, depression, and stress that piled up inside me, the faster I lashed out whenever I got upset. Everything felt like a fight. It felt like the whole world was attacking me.

When there were people around that I could blame for what I was feeling, I reacted with anger. But when it was just me, alone, on the inside I felt something much darker and lonelier. I felt hopeless. I was back on the edge of that big black hole of sadness I'd felt since I was a kid, just feeling lost, alone, miserable, and miles away from any hope of happiness.

How was it ever going to get better? What change could I make that would matter? I couldn't see a damn thing I could do that would make an impact on how far down my life had gotten. I had already lost what was most important to me. Even if I straightened up everything as good as I possibly could, stopped taking pills, and started acting the way everybody seemed to think I should, would that get me custody of my daughter back? Would that get me my relationship with her father back? Everything was still going to be messed up no matter what I did. The media was going to keep picking my every move apart no matter what. I'd never act perfect enough to change people's minds at that point. And even if I did, I'd still have that monster of depression and anxiety eating me up from the inside out every single day. The fact was I couldn't see a single exit from that moment in time that led to a better place. I felt like I was already so deep in the hole there was no point clawing at the walls. I was stuck at the bottom, and I just couldn't picture myself ever getting out.

And you want to know what? That wasn't just my take on the situation. If you followed the tabloids or read what people were saying online about me at the time, you would have seen plenty of people saying I was hopeless, worthless, selfish, a psychopath, a manipulator, a bully, a mess. And you would have seen plenty of people saying I should kill myself.

It had all come back around again. Just like that time when I was eleven years old and got so tired of feeling bad for no reason that I decided to do whatever I could to end it, I drifted into those desperate measures again. For the second time in my life, I went into the bathroom of my house and tried to hang myself.

Before I did it, I called up Leah's dad and told him I loved him. As shocking as it sounds, I barely remember any of this happening. It's like a movie playing in my head, little clips of it, because I was so checked out and blacked out. I didn't even take as many pills that day as I usually took. But it was just like, "I'm a failure. What's my purpose? I'm not even a mom. I don't have my family. I'm here all alone. What am I doing with my life?" Everything just seemed worthless. I didn't feel happy. I didn't feel any happiness at all. One sign that depression has grown out of control is when the things that usually bring you happiness or pleasure suddenly leave you feeling nothing at all. You love chocolate chip cookies? Not anymore. Best friend surprises you with an awesome present? You can't even pretend to be happy. Nothing feels real. Your good emotions have completely disappeared. That's where I was, to the point where even spending time with Leah wasn't giving me any sense of happiness, not even for a little bit. And that's bad. That's really bad. When I realized how far away I'd gotten from any chance of happiness, I just sort of said, "Fuck it, what's the point?"

I took a bunch of pills and tried to get a rope around my neck. I can't even remember clearly exactly what I did. When the police came, I was unconscious, just moaning. They put me on oxygen and took me the hospital, and I ended up regaining consciousness and stabilizing.

It was a very weak, weak point in my life. There's no question I needed some kind of extreme intervention at that moment. It just so happened that in order to avoid jail time for those battery charges, I had to agree to more intervention than I ever wanted. Specifically, the court ordered me to serve two years probation, invest ten thousand dollars in a college fund for Leah, and serve thirty days of anger management treatment in an inpatient rehab facility.

So just ten days after my fresh suicide attempt, I headed for rehab in Malibu, California. Pretty good timing, right? Ultimately, I didn't get much out of rehab because I was so resistant. At the time, I was completely convinced that I did not have a problem. Because they were prescriptions, and because I did feel so insane and anxious when I wasn't on anything, and because my rehab papers said I was only in there for anger management, it was easy for me to convince myself that I wasn't really an addict at all. I always had what felt like pretty solid excuses to fall back on, and I didn't have anywhere near the desire or motivation I needed to have to start fighting with the pills.

I did meet some great people in there. I made friends with an incredible fashion designer, a beautiful girl, and a wonderful person. And there was another girl, Molly, who I became amazing friends with. She was this beautiful California blond bombshell, very young and really fun. We did everything together in there, wearing each others clothes and hanging out all the time. There was one time, too, when one of the MTV producers came and saw me at rehab, and we went out and got our nails done and stuff. I even had a guy in there, which isn't remotely allowed in rehab. He was very cute and we had an amazing little romance in there. We never had sex, but we definitely broke the rules.

Rehab was only supposed to last for thirty days, but I ended up staying for sixty. I wasn't having fun, though. I had a social life and everything, I guess, but I also had some screaming matches with staff. I wasn't getting much of anything I actually needed out of the experience, obviously, not that it was anybody else's fault. And I was missing Leah so bad my heart was just aching. Her dad brought her out one time to visit, and that was a really good day. But the rest of the time I was just miserable and missing her and missing my family.

About two days before I left rehab I finally admitted I had a problem with pills. But I was already on my way out, so what were they going to do about it?

The day you leave rehab, they give you all your medication. Everything that's yours goes home with you. Right before I walked out of there, I got my pills and took five Klonopin. Sounds like a lot, huh? The sad thing is that was nothing to me.

I barely even remember flying home, although I do remember getting in a fight with a girl at the airport. There was a drunk couple there who started messing with my bodyguard, asking ignorant questions, and then they started yelling at me and stuff. Nothing serious happened, but that's pretty much what I remember of the trip home.

Which sums it up, basically. In my memory, that part of my life is just a dull haze punctuated by stupid shit.

When I got home, my mom was there, and she'd cleaned the house and put up a welcome home banner for me, which was really sweet. At this point, what everybody hoped was that I was on the road to recovery. That's what rehab is supposed to symbolize, after all. It was supposed to be a fresh start or a new beginning or whatever.

Obviously, reality was a little bit different. The stress of coming back from rehab just had me feeling like I needed more pills than ever. My ex-fiancé and I were fighting as bad as before, or maybe even worse. And something was starting to happen where I would black out for three days straight. I mean, I would literally look around on Wednesday and realize I didn't know how I got there from Monday. Any addicts out there will know what I'm talking about. There comes a point where you're so messed up on pills, and so *used* to being messed up on pills, that you start losing big chunks of time. The freaky thing is that you're still functioning and talking to people, but afterward you can't remember a damn thing. It's like something else has taken over your body while you've been asleep.

Like I said before, nobody came right out and confronted me on the pills or anything. But when a person changes as much as I had changed at that time, everybody around them notices. People were worried about me at the time, I know.

My mom and brother tried to reach out to me and talk about it, but even if we were talking, they couldn't reach me. Whenever anybody brought anything up, I'd shut it down. Part of the reason you don't hear much about my family as I tell this story is that I was always putting distance between me and them, especially as my situation got worse. Maybe I didn't want to face their questions. Maybe I just couldn't focus on anyone. Who knows? I doubt it will ever make perfect sense. I don't know how else to explain it other than that I was in a dark place.

My brother said to me later that he thought he had lost me at that point. Between the suicide attempt, the pills, and how detached I was from my life, he just thought I'd gone out of reach. After I got out of jail, we sat down and talked, and he looked me in the eye and said to me, "Amber, I'm not gonna lose my sister again." There's no question there were people around who loved me, and they weren't giving up on me. I was just on my own. If you ever met somebody who didn't give a shit, it was me. I didn't care about anything that happened anymore.

9

Nothing Left to Lose

Like any regular person out there, I've been diagnosed with my share of mental disorders over the years.

I'm just kidding. I know it's not really normal to have to use your fingers to count how many disorders you've heard in doctors' offices and counselors' rooms. Bipolar disorder, clinical depression, anxiety, sociopathic tendencies . . .

You know, I have to call a time out on that last one. Most of the time, I've been able to see where people were coming from. The anxiety is just a fact. I don't think you have to be a psychiatrist to see that much. Obviously depression is something I've struggled with since I was just a kid, so I have no argument there. Bipolar disorder? I don't know about that one, but I can understand how somebody might look at my behavior from, say, back when I was on the show and come up with that diagnosis. Half the time it looked like I was either screaming at my ex-fiancé or lying in bed. Manic-depressive. I get it. Whatever. Maybe.

But a sociopath? Come on.

Maybe the doctor who told me that thought I seemed unemotional. But maybe that had something to do with how many pills I was on at the time. I mean, how can you judge somebody's emotional reactions when they're on a prescribed cocktail of opiates, antidepressants, and anxiety medications? Of course I'm not going to be reacting to things like a normal person.

And, well, maybe I haven't always reacted to things the same way other people have. It's true I can remember a whole lot of times in my life when I didn't show the emotions people expected me to show. Even just off the top of my head, I can think of plenty of times where something horrible, shocking, or violent happened in front of me, and the other people who were there turned to me afterward and couldn't understand how calm I was. That's just the way I am. I don't always cry at funerals. I don't always freak out when something scary happens in front of me. And when I'm in a relationship, my heart doesn't always jump into it right away.

I can't explain all of that. I'm not the psychiatrist. But what I can say is that just because I'm not crying doesn't mean I'm not sad. Just because I'm not flipping out doesn't mean I'm not scared. And if I've been a little distant in my relationships, well, the fact is I'm still pretty young, and most of my memories are taken up by the one great big love that blew me away when I was sixteen, the love that gave me my daughter.

When I wasn't with Leah's father, I went through men like a hurricane. I never felt any deep feelings for these guys, even when they were really great. It just never stirred the same place inside me as my relationship with Leah's father. The stages of my life I went through with him were so intense:

falling in love for the first time, having sex for the first time, moving in together, having a child, and dealing with all the weirdness of getting famous from an MTV reality show. He was part of everything that happened to me, just like I was part of everything that happened to him. We were completely together. It's just impossible to think of those years without thinking of him. It's even hard to think about who I am or what my life is without him, because he's attached to all of those memories.

So honestly, I believe that's the reason I didn't get too emotional with those other guys. Not because I'm a damn sociopath.

Anyway, it's not like nobody's ever moved me since him. There was one guy who really made a mark on me after Leah's father, and he stuck by me more than almost anyone else through the next lowest point of my life.

Yeah, the next lowest point. That's right. Trust me, we haven't hit the bottom yet.

◆

To catch up on where we are now, this was the situation. I wasn't with Leah's father, and I didn't have Leah. And whenever I couldn't see her, my life was just parties, pills, and sex. I couldn't go out enough. I was drinking with paparazzi, going out with friends, hitting up the bars, and acting crazy. I was beyond all thoughts of rehab. I was just filling my nights with all the crazy shit I could pack in.

One night, I dragged my friend Sallie out to this bar called Jimmy's, and we were talking and drinking and having fun when these two dudes walked in with a girl.

One of these guys was fucking hot. He was just chiseled to

the core. Like a country boy with the body of a Greek god, I swear to you, and these beautiful blue eyes! I noticed him as soon as he walked in. He and his group started playing pool behind us, and I just kept carrying on with him in the corner of my eye, just admiring this gorgeous man. At some point, after awhile, Sallie had said something really funny and I turned away from her and let out this stupid giggle—and at the same time I caught his eye. It was the funniest little moment. I don't know how it worked.

But this beautiful guy walked up to me, pulled up a chair, and started talking. Right away there was this spark of chemistry between us like hardly anything I'd ever felt before. His name was Dan.

We ended up going home that night and making out, and everything about it was so unusual and awesome. We didn't even have sex that night. We ended up waiting for two weeks, which was a little unusual for me at the time—not to pull another shocker on you or anything. But when we finally did, it was like magic. Our connection was so perfect and insane; we just let loose and went wild with each other like neither of us had ever done with anybody before that. I remember afterward, we were just looking at each other in complete surprise. That's how good it was.

I don't know how I got together with this guy at the time I did. Dan was so sweet and so genuine, he balanced me out as much as anybody could have at a time when I had gone so crazy. I really needed what he gave me. We ended up getting together and having a beautiful relationship. We were so happy. We never fought. We made love five times a day, whenever we could. It was insane. Perfect, really.

There was never any drama with him. I remember one time we went to dinner and then wound up at some bar, and

I was out dancing with the DJ on the floor. That might have bothered another guy. Dan just stood on the side laughing, having a good time with me. There wasn't any jealousy, just fun and affection and this kind of classic all-American romance, or something. That night we drove my Lincoln through the field between our apartments to get back to his place and spend the night together. We were so passionate, it was almost like nothing else I've ever had. It was hot. It was beautiful. It was just the perfect chemistry.

But if you can get a sense of what kind of guy he was from the way I describe him, a good country boy with a sweet personality, you can see the obvious problem. It definitely doesn't take a rocket scientist. He was a good influence on me, but I was already beyond reach. There was just no stopping how wild I was at that point, and I was definitely too wild for him. I was taking everything so far at the time it would have tested anybody's limits. I wasn't partying like a normal person. I wasn't having sex like a normal person. Everything I was doing was extreme by default.

I didn't even mean to shock him as much as I did sometimes. There were things I did to hang out that I just thought were fun, but when I'd bring him along and see his reaction I'd actually see the gap in craziness there was between us. One night when Dan called me after work, I happened to be out with a bunch of guy friends at a strip club. You know, just the regular stuff you do when your boyfriend's at work. Dan was so easygoing, it wasn't the kind of thing that could freak him out or make him upset. So what did I do? I called him to come over and join us.

When Dan got to the strip club, he looked so nervous it was adorable. I was just cracking up watching him take the place in. It was obvious he didn't know how to deal with being in the same room as a bunch of naked women and his girlfriend at the same time. The poor kid didn't know where to look, and it was cracking me up. And then, obviously, I had to take it further. I just couldn't resist! I turned to him and said, "Hey, let's go get a private dance." Dan looked at me like I was completely insane, but at that point I think he just didn't know what to do other than go with it.

We went to the little back area where they had a couch with a mirror behind it, and we sat next to each other to get the dance. I was a little bit excited because it was my first time doing something like that with a guy, but I wasn't exactly that far out of my element at that time. The dancer was actually a friend of mine, as a matter of fact. So it was definitely even more of a crazy experience for him. She did her thing on me first, putting my hands on the sides of her body and all of that good stuff. And then she'd move over to him and try to do the same. But this kid was so sweet, he snatched his hands back and practically sat on them. He was looking at me all wide-eyed like he was going to get in trouble. I was like, "Dude, it's okay—I'm paying!"

The boy could not handle my life. Can't blame him.

Besides that, though, we had a beautiful connection. It was even good enough to withstand all the bombs that started going off as a result of my addiction and my behavior. There were fun and games on the surface, but I was still on the same steady slide toward self-destruction I'd been on for the last few years. The amazing thing about Dan was that he stuck by my side for as long as he did. He was a sweet person and a gentleman all the way through. I will never forget how considerate he was. In another life, I think we could have had something special. Unfortunately, we weren't cut out for making it together in this one.

When I was with Dan, I was still on probation from when I was charged with assaulting Leah's dad. That meant I had regular appointments with a probation officer, and I had to take urine tests basically whenever they wanted me to, to show I wasn't on drugs.

There was a problem with the urine tests, though. Not a problem for me, exactly, but a problem for anybody who was interested in getting me clean and sober. The thing was, all the drugs I was taking were prescriptions. I wasn't smoking weed or shooting up or anything. I was abusing pills I'd gotten from doctors, which meant nothing was showing up on those pee tests that I wasn't actually supposed to be on. I was allowed to be on Klonopin, for example, and no test could tell them whether I was taking one or five at a time. It couldn't tell them if I was getting more pills from the street to kick up what I was supposed to be taking. Basically, the pee tests were pretty pointless in relation to what my actual problem was.

Let's take a minute to talk about how I ended up on so many drugs in the first place. It's actually one of the easier sets of facts to pin down, believe it or not. It all started with my first visit to the clinic in Anderson, where I got my first prescription for Klonopin. That was prescribed to me for my anxiety, which was getting to be crippling at the time. I wasn't diagnosed with anything, formally, when I got that prescription. I hadn't seen a psychiatrist, so there was no way to get a diagnosis at the clinic.

A doctor diagnosed me with bipolar disorder, which pretty much guarantees you're going to go through a whole lot of meds. The nature of the illness is that you swing between periods of extreme highs and lows, and you have to find a way to medicate them both without pushing the scale too far either way. Like most people who get told they have bipolar disorder, I tried almost everything that's normally prescribed for it, and the only one that worked for me as an anti-depressant was Cymbalta.

The Klonopin wasn't doing what it was supposed to do for me, and I was still having a seriously difficult time dealing with the anxiety, depression, and the other symptoms they were chalking up to bipolar disorder. I ended up getting prescribed Vistaril and Lithium, as well, to deal with that.

More medication was added to the menu when the doctor finally checked out my back and told me the insane amount of pain I was having was caused by scoliosis. That led to me being prescribed Soma, a muscle relaxer, and Hydrocodone, a painkiller. My complaints about the back stuff might be easy for people to roll their eyes at, but it is serious. My brother has a similar problem, and actually has to get shots to deal with the pain in his back. It's horrible pain, sometimes to the point where you can barely move.

I can't blame the doctor for letting me have what I looked like I needed. The thing is, as an addict, you really play the game and do the acting part when you talk to your doctor. It's really what any addict does when they find themselves with a doctor. They overact, overreact, and milk the most out of anything they can just to get more and more of what they actually think they need. That's exactly what I was doing, and I think unfortunately I was pretty damn good at it. So I can't blame the person who wrote the prescriptions. The man thought I really needed these things, and he thought I was doing everything I was supposed to.

Or maybe it's not so simple. I don't know. It's hard to look back and honestly believe it wasn't obvious I was messed up on those pills. But what do I know? I mean, I was messed up on pills.

I will say this: the people who are usually prescribed the hardcore medications like Oxycontin and Hydrocodone are cancer patients or people who are dealing with serious chronic pain. Those are the kinds of cases where you can look at a person and get a pretty good idea that they need to be on something like Oxy. The people who get it for back pain, for the most part, have to diagnose themselves. But Hydrocodone is a drug you're supposed to take for seriously painful back problems, and it is effective. It's just a problem of whether you abuse it or not. I was abusing it. I was taking eight in a handful every three hours if I wanted to. How was the doctor going to stop me from doing that? There's only so much even authorities can do to protect you from yourself. My addiction just wasn't the kind that was easy for doctors to prevent. It wasn't even the kind a pee test could always catch.

Still, I had to follow the rules and pee when they told me to pee, meet my officer when they told me to meet my officer. And breaking those rules was what got me busted.

Like my ex-fiancé, Dan wasn't a fan of the pills. I don't think he ever touched one in his life. All he ever did was drink, and he only did that like a normal guy. The pills had no appeal for him.

One night he came upstairs and found me passed out on the bed with a bottle of them right beside me. When he saw me laying there, he was so scared he started freaking out, shaking me, and trying to figure out if he should call 911 or something. I guess I did something to reassure him. I only remember waking up at four-thirty in the morning and giving it to him, which just goes to show you how adjusted I'd become to that way of life. That I could take so many pills that my boyfriend thought I was on the brink of death, and then wake up and want to do it. How crazy is that? Scaring the shit out of somebody and then waking up and just having sex? I don't know what was going on in my head.

Unfortunately, even though I was apparently able to wake up for sex, I wasn't able to wake up for my appointment with my probation officer.

I must have been completely out that morning. The officer said she was banging on the door for ten minutes before I finally dragged my ass out of bed and opened the door. The first thing she said was I'd missed my appointment and I needed to do a pee test.

The thing is, I never really got the hang of peeing on command. And that morning, I literally couldn't pee. Once again, the ironic thing is that nothing bad would have shown up on that test if I'd been able to take it. All I was doing was buying more of the same opiates I was prescribed. I would have gotten away with it. But I just couldn't pee.

So the probation officer started looking around my house, and it was a matter of minutes before she found the extra pills I'd stashed in my purse under the bed. That was that. I could hear the hammer coming down.

I asked her if I was going to jail for this, and she gave me the kind of vague answer that told me exactly what the deal was. I went straight off to tell my family and friends: "Hey, guys. I'm going to jail."

They didn't believe me, but I wasn't an idiot. I could read between the lines, and it turned out I was right. They gave me a date to come to the courthouse and pretty much check myself in for three months at county.

Three months in jail. God. I'd had a taste of county early on when the battery charges were brought against me, but I'd only been in there for twenty-four hours, and I was too out of it to really get much of an impression of it. Three months, though? I couldn't wrap my head around it. In fact I'm not even sure I tried. At the time, I thought I was still going to get out of it somehow, the way I almost always get out of everything.

But probation's no joke, and those pills had sealed my fate. Somewhere deep down, I kind of knew I was screwed. As the day got closer and closer, I just kept myself in a haze where I didn't really have to deal with it. Maybe I literally couldn't deal with it at that point.

Surprisingly enough, or not surprisingly considering what a sweet guy he was, Dan spent that whole last night with me. We just stayed up hanging out while I enjoyed my last taste of freedom before I went behind bars. I'd describe what that felt like to know I was about to head into a place I'd never expected to go into, but I was still in such a haze of pills it was hardly even real. I just know Dan and I hung out that night and enjoyed every minute, soaking up each other's company for as long as we could.

And then off I went to the courthouse.

One thing I will never forget is the outfit I was wearing when I headed into county. I walked into that courthouse wearing five-inch glitter pumps and my long white Jackie O coat, topped off with an off-white knit ski cap with flaps on the side. Talk about not giving a shit. Imagine somebody handcuffed to a chair in the courthouse in that get-up! I definitely did not present the image of somebody who was taking that shit very seriously. For what it's worth, though, I must have made an impression on the sheriff and all the people at the courthouse, because they are all very sweet to me now. I guess sometimes you just can't argue with glitter.

Not that I ever wanted to get on such good terms with that crew. When I walked in, I had every intention of paying my bond and getting the hell out of there. I just needed a lawyer to fix me up. All these guys in suits kept walking by, and I sort of called out to one of them like, "Psst! Hey, come here!"

The lawyer walked up to me, and I leaned toward him and said, "Listen, I'm in a lot of shit, and I need you to get me out. This is jail, and I do not want to be here. Get me out. My name is . . . "

"I know who you are."

Name recognition at the county courthouse. That's one way to be famous, huh?

"Okay," I said. "Well, get me out."

That was when the sheriff rustled a few papers and dropped the bomb.

"You don't have a bond."

Talk about a punch in the gut. I didn't have a bond. Which meant there was no paying my way out. There was no way around it. Since the first day the state caught wind of me through the show, it seemed like people had been trying to send me to prison, and everybody who had my back had fought hard to keep me out of it. But I had finally crossed the line. I was screwed.

I was going to jail.

10

Crash Landing

Walking into county for a three-month sentence must be a really shocking experience. I mean, that must really freak a person out, walking up those stairs with all of these crazy bitches banging on the doors and screaming and laughing, freaking out and yelling, "Hey, *Teen Mom! Teen Mom!*"

Seriously, it must be weird. I can't really tell you from personal experience, though, because I was so high when I walked into county jail, I couldn't really process anything. Nothing was real to me yet. But it was going to get real pretty soon.

Remember all those prescriptions I was on? After a few years of being prescribed medications, legitimately, for depression, anxiety, and back pain, I'd designed a pretty serious cocktail for myself. I never doctor shopped for more prescriptions, because I had plenty. But what I would do is supplement the pills from the pharmacy with more of the same pills from the street. That was what kept me in supply so I could keep gobbling them up the way I was doing.

Pills, pills, pills. I know. But let's break down what this means a little further in terms of what I was doing to my body. I weighed about a hundred and fifteen pounds, and every day, about every four to six hours, I was taking eight or ten of my ten-milligram Hydros, which is an unholy amount of those to take. Then I was rounding it out with three Klono-pins, two Valiums, and a Soma. I'm going to go out on a limb here and say you don't have to be a drug addict or an expert to realize that's a hell of a handful. But I'd down that cocktail every day, and then there would be times that I'd forget I took certain pills and end up taking more than I could handle and getting sick to my stomach. That's another dangerous thing about being a pill-head, forgetting what pills you take and then taking more. It's pretty terrible and can end very bad. I pushed my body way too far on several occasions by doing that, to the point where I knew without a doubt I was lucky to wake up alive.

Anyway, that was the menu I was living on when I went into jail. And any doctor will tell you, that's not something you can stop cold turkey.

One of the most notorious things about opiates, and the reason why they are so serious, is the fact that once you're on them it's very difficult, physically, to get off of them. Someone who's been on those painkillers for a long time has to be careful getting off of them, because it's such a shock to the system. Usually a doctor supervises the process. Coming off of opiates is no joke, and I became the poster child for that fact the day after I went behind bars and started going into withdrawal.

I don't think anybody can understand the feeling of withdrawals if you haven't had them. It's not a fever. It's not a sickness. It's hell. It's death. I literally felt like I was going to die. I started having these sort of seizures, and the nurses ran in and stuck something in my nose. I woke up shaking horrendously and sick to my stomach, feeling like my body was about to explode out of my skin. I felt like somebody might as well have poisoned me, tortured me, and buried me alive. I've never felt anything that bad in my life. I was puking my guts out, I had diarrhea, I couldn't eat anything, and I couldn't even get up to take a shower.

A small bit of luck I had was that I got assigned to a block with two really sweet, kindhearted girls who took me under their wings. They took care of me for the first week I was detoxing, bringing me food and checking in on me all the time. It took about two to three weeks to get it all out of my system. In the middle of it, when I was detoxing really bad, I had a court appearance over a TV monitor where the judge dashed any hopes I had of rescue and told me I wasn't going anywhere. I would have to stay in jail until they found out what the next trial date for me was. That absolutely killed me.

I didn't cry, though. I'm not a big crier under normal circumstances, and I didn't shed a tear for a pretty long time in jail. But when I did, I really did. It was December when I went in, just in time for the holidays, and if you want to hear three of the most depressing words in the English language, I'll offer you, "Christmas in jail."

When Christmas came around, these volunteers came in to visit us. They were older women from a church or a nursing home or something. They come around for the holidays and visit each block to pass out cookies and sing songs. It was something like eight women who came to my block, and they gave us the cookies and they were as sweet as they could possibly be. Then they started singing their song. They sang that we all had hope, that we all had a chance. I just started bawling.

After about a month in there I started getting used to everybody and made a lot of friends. There were still some people talking smack. I knew some girls in there from growing up together, and some of them wouldn't let go of the whole *Teen Mom* thing. A girl was kicked out of our room for stealing my stuff, and I had some close calls where I almost got into a few fights. But I had my allies in there, just enough really cool girls who stuck together and got each other through that horrible experience.

After I was done detoxing, I was totally clean and sober for the first time in a long while. I hate to disappoint you, but there were no blue skies or angels singing that went along with it. Being sober in jail was hell. It sucked. It's different to be clean and to be out in a good environment, when you've had time to make the right decisions for yourself and get in the mindset you need to be. But it wasn't like I detoxed and woke up in a field of daisies, or even a comfortable bed. I repeat: being sober in jail sucked.

This is what it's like to be an addict, and this is why it's so hard to force somebody to get off of drugs before they make that choice for themselves: I felt like it was the time when I needed those drugs the most, and I didn't have them. That was the only way I looked at it, and it was a very helpless, very low feeling. I couldn't see anything good about being clean. Nothing. The worst part of it, which is obviously a lot clearer to me now, is that I'd been mixing up the pills I really needed with the pills I was abusing for so long that I didn't know how to take care of myself at all. Those doctors weren't just prescribing me all of those pills for fun. It might have been too much, maybe—you think? But I *do* have anxiety. I *do* have depression. I *do* have scoliosis and back pain that literally stops me from moving sometimes. Basically, I did need to be on medication, and I probably still do. But I messed with it for so long that I became a drug addict, and I completely lost perspective on how much I needed the pills, and how much of them I needed, and which ones I needed. I had gone so extreme that I had no concept of the right middle ground. So when I went to jail and I didn't have that ridiculous cocktail anymore, I felt totally overwhelmed by the feeling of having absolutely *nothing* to help me cope with the worst situation I had ever been in.

I never wanted to be in jail! That wasn't a plan I had for myself at any point in my life. It wasn't something I ever even remotely considered happening to me. And yet there I was, sitting in jail, locked up and pissed off, hating sobriety, and having absolutely no sense of hope that my situation was going to get any better.

What could have gotten through to me at that time? I spend a lot of time thinking about that now. Someone as stubborn as I was, who had pushed the limits so far and gotten away with so much and was so intent on doing what she was doing, how do you get through to a person like that and help them onto a better road?

Usually the next step is a halfway house. I don't know if that would have done anything for me or not, but I never got the chance to try it. Why? The halfway houses wouldn't take me. That makes me angry to this day. I was locked up, I was sober, and to stay that way I needed every ounce of help I could get. But it came down through the grapevine that the halfway houses were refusing to take me because they thought my "celebrity status" was going to be bad for the other girls. There are no words for how upset that makes me, especially now that I am sober and educated enough to understand that you *never* deny someone their sobriety.

I had no hope. And that whole saga kept me in jail for an extra week, by the way. Because I didn't get into any halfway houses, I wound up on house arrest and in drug court. Please take this as my own personal opinion: drug court is dumb. Basically, you have to wake up every single morning at six-thirty to go to their designated place and pee. And if you can't pee, you're in big trouble. Which sucks for me, because like I said, I just can't pee on command. I don't know. Just never got the hang of it. It's not one of my talents. I had to dip back into jail not once, but twice for not being able to pee. And not because I was afraid of the test results, but because there was some woman sitting there a foot away from me, staring at me. I'd get nervous and not pee, and then I'd get sanctioned and have to go into jail for a week.

It was so stupid, because seriously, I was still out of reach of those pee tests. In fact, as soon as I got out of jail, I got into a new drug that they couldn't detect. And this drug was trouble.

♦

When I was in jail, I became really good friends with a girl named Sally. She got out of there a week before I did, and she was in the same situation as me with house arrest and drug court. About a week after I got out, I ran into her at drug court. It was one of the days when I couldn't make it happen, and I was sitting outside drinking water, which they served me in a clean pee cup, by the way—thanks. Sally walked in and we said hi and exchanged numbers, which is completely not allowed, for reasons that became clear pretty much immediately.

Sally texted me to hang out later, and when she came by and picked me up, the first thing she said was, "Wanna get high?"

I looked at her like she was crazy, like, "How is that even possible?"

"Man," she said, "Fentanyl patches. It doesn't show up on the drug thing."

"Fuck yeah," I said.

Before I knew it, we were sitting in a park, and she was giving me this tiny little dot of paper. I looked at it and said, "What the hell is that?" I was thinking about the piles of pills I'd gotten used to before I went into jail. "That's not gonna do anything for me."

She was like, "Trust me."

Fentanyl is serious business. It's a serious, serious pain-killer. It comes in a patch, like a nicotine patch or something, that you're supposed to put on your body and wear for days so your body gets the pain relief slow and steady, like an IV drip. Obviously it's for people who have extreme pain to deal with, like cancer breakthrough pain, and it can even be used to keep people sedated. Fentanyl just does not fuck around. Dose for dose, it's about fifty to a hundred times more powerful than morphine.

Not many people know about it, I guess. I didn't for a long time. I wish I hadn't found out. But I put the little dot on my finger and put it in my mouth, and in forty-five minutes, I was gone.

It was the worst thing that could have happened to me at that time. I fell in love with those things so hard I became an addict on a completely different level. Until then it seemed like I'd been racing to rock bottom as fast as I could. These things were like the turbo blast that took me there instantly. Sally would pick me up every morning and take me to drug court to go and do the pee tests, and everybody in there knew we were breaking the rules by hanging out. They'd smile and shake their heads when we walked in together. I'm guessing they probably wouldn't have taken it so lightly if they'd known I was chewing on those patches while I was peeing.

I got into those Fentanyl patches so bad. I just couldn't get enough. I'd tear off those little pieces of the patches keep them in my cheek, and nobody had any idea. It's very scary to think about that, that I could have something that strong, and that addictive, and that easy to get away with.

Obviously I didn't get away with it forever, and the day finally came when I did too much at the wrong time. Sally and I were on our way to IOP, or intensive outpatient class, which is a type of counseling program for new recovering addicts. She was driving us in her car. I was so high I was lying down in the seat, and at every turn I was going, "I'm too high. I'm too high." She was laughing at me at first, but before long she was pulling over and I was puking on the side of the road. I mean, I know the difference between high and too high. And I was *way* too high to function. But you can't miss IOP. That's not how it works when they let you out of prison. You don't just get to skip things when you don't feel well. So we had no choice but to try and get through it.

It did not work out well for me. Soon enough I was sitting there in IOP, nodding out, which means passing in and out of consciousness in a way that's obviously caused by taking too much of something. In front of the teacher, with fifteen other people sitting in a circle so everybody sees everybody, I was drifting off and swaying in my chair, making it as obvious as possible that I had found myself some drugs to get messed up on.

Nobody said anything that day, but they didn't have to. I had gone too far. The show was winding down.

I had fought like a motherfucker to keep doing what I was doing. I did not care what obstacles stood between me and the things I wanted to do, and so far I hadn't run into one I couldn't find a way to get around. Nothing in drug court worked for me. Jail didn't work for me. Narcotics Anonymous didn't work for me. The people involved in these programs and the people who were trying to force me into sobriety were relentless, but I was more relentless than they were. It had reached a point where every bit of strength I had, I put into my addiction. And anything that tried to stand in my way, I either knocked it down or found a way to tunnel underneath it.

I didn't care. Period. I did not care. It was like, "Put me on house arrest, put me in drug court, and I'll show you what I can do. Tell me I can't hang out with this girl from jail, and she'll be at my house every day. Tell me I have to wake up every morning to take a pee test, and I'll walk in with an even stronger drug hidden in my cheek." Whenever I had to face some consequence or limit to my actions, it was like it became some twisted challenge to me. I was fighting a battle of my own making, and for what? To see how much more messed up I could get than I already was?

Where was Leah, you ask? Good question. She was safe and sound. But she was not with me.

I was so deep into my addiction that I wasn't seeing my daughter at all. Her father and I didn't have a good relationship, and that's putting it lightly. We were about as far from co-parenting as it gets. Feeling better and fixing up my life had become the farthest thing from my mind. It was like everything got turned upside-down, and I was literally fighting to keep myself messed up—even if I didn't exactly see it that way at the time.

When you don't want to be present anymore, when you don't want to have any emotions and all you want to be is numb—if that's the reason why you're taking all of those pills—the fact is you just don't care. It's really hard for people on the outside to understand what that feels like. That's a good thing, obviously, because you don't want everybody to be walking around in a daze, not giving a shit about anything. But it's frustrating to try and explain what the experience is like, because most normal people will never find themselves in that state of mind. It's hard to look someone in the eye and convince them of your love and concern when you both know there was a time when you were able to completely shut them out of your mind and heart. It's even hard to explain it to yourself, once it's over. Even when you're the one who went through it, it's hard to make sense of that mindset once you've gotten better and learned how to care again.

But the fact is, when you are that low, when you are that deep into addiction, you just don't care. And that's one of the most dangerous positions to be in in the world.

Sally disappeared for a little while when she had to go back to jail for some sanction. All of a sudden, I was really fucking tired. Maybe something had been shifting inside of me for a while, but at that time I found myself feeling miserable in a whole new way. I had just gotten surgery to have my gallbladder taken out, and it left me feeling completely wrecked. Physically I felt weak, and mentally I felt weak. All at once it was like I could actually feel myself deteriorating.

When Sally got back out and came over to my house, it took me three minutes to get her to give me pills. She gave me a bunch of Suboxone, which was on a completely different level to anything I'd been doing. Over the next three days, I took thirty pills.

I shouldn't be alive right now. Nobody knows how I made it. I remember taking a handful of pills, nodding out, waking up, and taking more. Every time I'd nod out and wake up and take more, over and over, for three days.

It sounds like I was trying to die. I wasn't thinking about it explicitly, but I had definitely given up on myself. It was like, "If I wake up, cool. Maybe there's a reason for it. If I don't wake up, cool. It's not gonna bother me."

I did wake up, and I was as shocked as anyone else would have been. I was dazed. I didn't even know how I'd survived it. I was so close to death. And I have been there before, more times than I wish, and probably more times than I know about. But this time, it flipped a switch somewhere inside of me that nothing and no one else had been able to reach. Suddenly, I had had enough.

I knew if I was going to change, something extreme needed to happen. At that point it didn't even matter what that was. I barely had enough left in me to think straight, but I knew I couldn't stand this situation anymore. It had gotten to the point where I could feel just enough of that deep fear I keep deep inside, the fear of looking back and regretting the choice I didn't make.

I had to take control. I had to change my life. I had to make a decision.

That morning I had to go to court, and I called up Leah's father and begged him to go with me. He didn't understand why. Nobody had any idea what I was planning. It was almost weird that he agreed to go in with me, considering our relationship at the time. Maybe he sensed something was different.

My behavior wasn't a secret anymore. I might have gotten away with the patches for awhile, but I don't think anybody gets away with nodding out in the middle of an IOP class. They were ready for me, and when I walked into court, I heard the full report on how bad I was doing. I just listened. It wasn't news to me.

And when it was my turn to speak, I told the judge I wanted to opt out of drug court. I said I wanted to take the alternative. I said I wanted to go to prison.

I remember the sound in the room was a big long gasp. But all I had to say was, "I can't do this anymore." The judge asked me if I knew I was sentenced to five years in prison if I opted out of treatment, and I said yes, I did. You're not usually allowed to have attorneys in drug court, but the judge made an exception for me. My lawyer came in and tried to talk me out of it, but I had already made up my mind. I told him, "There's not a program they can put me in that's gonna do anything. Take me to prison."

The decision shocked everyone, especially my friends and family. They were extremely upset. I remember seeing a photo of my ex-fiancé online from that day, and just being so caught off. I know that guy like the back of my hand, and I could see the devastation on his face. He was very worried and very sad. Later he told me that when MTV came by to talk to him about it, he got so depressed he went into his room, lay down, and slept all day.

At the time I wasn't thinking about whether it was a selfish choice or not. My mind still wasn't all there. It was almost like I was in shock that day. But to a lot of people it looked like

I was turning my back on them and running away; from my family, from my daughter, from my responsibilities. They had a hard time understanding why I couldn't just suck it up and deal with drug court and use the resources that were there to help me get sober. How could I explain it to them, though?

It's hard to live with yourself thinking about how you've let people down, and how bad you've hurt them. Especially when you know you will never really be able to explain to them why you did it, or why it was the only choice. I understand how they felt. It's hard to accept that somebody you love will be going to prison for years.

My ex-fiancé showed a lot of concern for me after I made that decision. When I talked to him afterward, he'd been calling up everyone he knew to find out what it all meant for me. He looked up all of these programs and ways to get my time cut. "Amber, you can do this, and you can do that, and you have to do this, and you can get out early, okay?"

I feel horrible when I think about it. It makes me think of how much I've hurt him and everyone around me. How low my life had gotten, where I felt I had to send myself to jail and be cut off from my daughter and my parents and everyone else because that was the only way I knew to get myself under control and away from death.

Since I've been out of prison, my whole family and Leah's father all say that now they understand. They see how the experience changed me and my life, and they're glad to see who I've become. But at the time, in the beginning, it was very painful and hurtful for them. I'm sure they still wish I could have accomplished what I accomplished in another way. It was extremely emotional all around, right up to the day I went back into county jail, where I waited to be transported to prison.

The first time the other inmates and I were set to move from county to prison, it was canceled at the last minute. My lawyer had slipped up and said something to the media about me leaving, and the prison called it a security threat and decided to change the schedule. The other girls were furious with me over that. In county, everyone's anxious to get to prison. County jail sucks. It's tiny, you wear these nasty uniforms, and you have to clean your clothes in the sink. Prison is bigger, and you can walk around and be outside. So the day the shuttle bus comes and takes you out of county, even though in one sense you're just getting out of the frying pan and into the fire, in another sense you're like, "God-damn, finally."

When the coast was clear and the prison felt safe from the paparazzi, or whatever they thought the security threat was, it was finally our time to go. The guards came in the morning and shackled us up all together, packed us into the van like sardines, and drove us off.

Driving up toward those gates, I felt numb.

What had I gone and done this time?

11

Shelter from the Storm

I wanted extreme, and I got it.

My *Teen Mom* reputation still caused me problems from the get-go. Almost as soon as I set foot on prison grounds, I heard they were thinking of putting me in solitary. For some reason, they still considered my whole situation some kind of security threat. Luckily, that didn't happen. But I still had a lot of crazy, screaming bitches to deal with. I was getting yelled at across the yard. People were cussing and calling me names, telling me I wasn't in kiddie camp anymore, telling me to put money on their books. They all knew who I was, and they'd all walk by mean-mugging and demanding to know what the fuck I was looking at. It was rough in there, and of course there's nothing you can do about it when that happens. You can't be a narc, or a snitch, or a pussy. You just have to put up with it and ride it out until you find some people you can deal with.

Fortunately, by the time we got out of intake and I made it to my dorm, I had met two girls, Lisa and Stephanie, who sort of ran their whole side of the place. They made it a point to hang out with me and watch my back. They were both gang members. Lisa had been in for ten years for shooting a girl. She wasn't some huge, tough-looking woman. She was very, very pretty and very kind and warm to me. Lisa and Stephanie were the first of many girls I wound up meeting behind bars who became close friends of mine. We spent a lot of time talking to each other about our situation. Like, how did we get to prison? What are we doing here?

We had a lot to talk about. One of the most depressing things in prison is being taken away from your family. There are so many women in jail who are separated from their kids. Their kids are taken away when they go to prison, moved in with relatives, or put into foster homes. It's a constant topic behind bars, these women missing their kids.

Now I was one of those women.

When the drugs wore off, I was finally alone with reality. It wasn't like the first time, in county, when I spent weeks destroyed by withdrawal and the rest of my time counting the days until I could get out and pick up my addiction right where I left off. This time was serious in a way none of the consequences had ever been. I was locked up with myself, and I was going to stay that way for a long, long time. I was alone in a way I had never been in my entire life.

The first thing I learned, and I learned it pretty quick, was that you never really know yourself until you're completely alone. My situation was miserable. There's no getting around that. But at the same time, I was clearheaded for the first time I could remember. It was like finding a safe place in the middle of a long war. It was a shitty safe place, with concrete walls and locked doors and gates and a bunch of people watching my every move, but it was a safe place all the same. Prison was a shelter from my addiction, and I had locked myself inside of it for the long haul.

Knowing where I was, knowing how long I'd be there, I was able—forced, really—to settle down and listen to my thoughts. For years, I'd been killing them with opiates, throwing handfuls of pills at my emotions to keep them away from me. Now I could feel everything, and I had to learn how to handle it all over again. I had to get to know myself almost from scratch.

I can't tell you how many nights I spent sitting on my bunk, looking around and seeing everyone else asleep. I was always the one who was awake until four in the morning. I've always been the most nocturnal person I know, so that by itself wasn't a big difference. But when you're alone at night in prison, you're alone with yourself. There's no TV to distract you. There are no phones in there to play with while you lie in bed. No computers. All you have is a pair of headphones and a radio.

But you find yourself when you're alone in thought, and that's what happened to me. Every night I was lying in bed, looking out the window, just turning everything over in my mind. It was a scary, humbling, terrifying experience. But after a few weeks, or a few months, I found myself thinking, "You know, I'm all right. I feel better today than I did a year ago, when I was free. So I'm okay."

It's a very powerful thing, having that time alone to think. I can't say enough about it. I sometimes wonder if I ever would have had that experience and that chance to learn and grow the way I did if I hadn't gone to prison. Even if there were no drugs and I was acting the way I was supposed to, I might have still kept jumping from relationship to relationship, never comfortable enough with myself to take that time to really think. And even if I had been comfortable enough, I never would have been in a situation where I had to examine my life and myself in such an intense way, with none of the distractions we have in our normal lives. Lying in that bunk, I couldn't even see the night sky because the lights in the yard were so bright. I literally had nothing to focus on but the thoughts in my mind.

You start to have these "Aha" moments. I can't give you the exact date or time that it happened, but one day, I just knew I was going to turn things around.

Since I was a kid, I've never found joy in living. I've always struggled just to feel okay. Everything was a fight against darkness. I spent years full of anger and hate over the things that were wrong with my life. I hated my childhood, the constant fighting, the drinking, the years with my father that I lost to his addiction and his sickness. All my life, my stomach turned when I thought of that terrible night when we lost my baby sister. It was so wrong, so horrible, and so unfair. I was angry at the way my family fell apart in the years afterward, the blame and bad feelings that tore everything up.

I grew up hating my life, hating my body, hating the darkness and loneliness I couldn't get out of my head. I spent a lot of time and energy turning that hatred on myself, from the first time I made myself throw up in grade school, to my first attempt at suicide at eleven, to the pills I abused without any concern for what I was doing to my mind and body. And when I couldn't keep that anger and hatred to myself anymore, it spilled over into the rest of my life and started to destroy everything.

I wonder how much my father can relate to my experience. When you look at the two of us, the similarities are undeniable. Until the day I went to prison, I was going down almost the exact same road he'd gotten stuck on in his life. What if I had kept going? What if Leah had gotten older and I had gotten worse? What if her happy memories of me and our special bond turned into the bitterness and anger of a child who loses her parent to addiction? Would the pills have turned her mom into a monster the way alcohol turned my dad into one?

I know now that my dad was fighting his own demons when I was growing up. Losing my baby sister, Candace, and then being blamed for her death, being blamed for the horrible death of his own daughter, is worse than anything real I've ever gone through. And who knows what else was inside his mind that made it hard for him to fight his alcoholism?

I understand his situation now more than ever. It doesn't give me back the years I lost with him, and that still breaks my heart. But I can learn from what my father and I have in common.

When my dad got sick and I spent those painful weeks with him, listening to him moaning in pain and praying not to die, I saw a man whose addiction had dragged him down to rock bottom. But in all that suffering, I also saw something truly amazing. After all that had happened, all the things he'd done to hurt me, he was able to look me in the eye with honest love and tell me that he was sorry. And even after all the damage he had done, all the hatred I thought I felt for him, I was able to forgive him. It wasn't too late. It's never too late.

Maybe my father was just like me. Maybe nothing could have helped him get back to himself except something unbelievably extreme. I wish to god he hadn't gotten sick. I wish more than anything the doctor hadn't said back then that he had only eight months to live. I wish I could know him healthy now, and look forward to many years together. But just like no regular kind of help, treatment, family intervention, or program was able to drag me away from my demons, I think my father just never came across the kind of help he needed.

I had. Prison was my help. That's what I knew, deep down, when I told the judge I wanted to take my jail sentence. Prison was the extreme thing I needed to get me off of the road I was following my dad down. And I'm lucky, I'm lucky as hell that I got off so much earlier than he did.

It wasn't too late for me. I knew it. I knew I was going to be okay. I can't tell you the exact date or time it happened, but one day I just knew I was going to take all that darkness, hatred, and anger I'd been fighting all my life and turn it around times ten. I was going to put all of that negative energy into the strength that would get me the fuck out of prison and into a life that was good and right.

Leah wasn't going to be an angry teenager, hating her mom for choosing addiction over motherhood. Leah was going to get her mom back. I was going to get my family back. That was my only focus, my only goal, and I was completely determined to use my time in prison to put everything I had into achieving it. And that's exactly what I did.

Those were the realizations I came up with when I was alone there in that miserable place. Those long nights alone in prison can tear you down, and for some people it does. But it can also build you up. And if you can face yourself like that, you can see that you can get through it. If you work your ass off, you can get through it. And when you put all that together, you will make yourself a stronger person.

♦

The CLIFF program helped me save my life in prison. CLIFF stands for "Clean Living is Freedom Forever," which is beautiful in itself. It's an amazing program that you live and breathe every minute of every day in there. What CLIFF basically is, is a college for addicts. You spend hours a day in tons of different classes, and you become a part of an extremely tight group of women who are doing the work right along with you. You almost feel like you're in a crazy sorority house sometimes. The program is led almost completely by inmates, with just a small number of counselors who sort of oversee everything and make sure everything is running the way it should. As you work your way through the meetings and classes, you get higher and higher in the program and take on more responsibilities. The women who have been in the program for the longest work as the facilitators and teachers, and they manage everything from the schedules to placing teachers in classes and sitting in on interviews and training.

It's kind of tragic I was such a bad student in school. The weird thing is I've always been really good at studying and helping other people study, when I put my mind to it. When Leah's father was preparing for his CNA test, I was the most devoted study partner around. I helped him drill through that material every night until he aced the exam. In prison it was the same thing. One of the big steps I needed to take in there was getting my GED. I knew if I passed my GED, I'd get my time cut automatically in half, so obviously that was a top priority. I teamed up with a friend and we studied our asses off for that GED. When everyone took the test, I had the number one score, and my study partner had number two.

My scores were so high they told me I would have been in the top ten of my graduating class if I'd performed like that in high school. If I had actually stuck with it, stayed in school and done right, I could have had a totally different story. But even if you can't change the past, it's never too late to take a turn toward something better. It's definitely never too late to act smart and work hard.

Along with the GED, I really put everything into the CLIFF program. I took anger management, and ended up *teaching* anger management. I took parenting classes, which wasn't even required. By the time I was out of prison, all of the facilitators and directors were my friends, and if anybody in the program had a question I was one of the few people they could always come to. I knew everything, and if I didn't, I'd figure it out. They called us the moms of the program.

There are so many women in prison who just need help. So many of them are just drug addicts who never even got the chance to get the help they needed before they wound up in prison. And at that point, they'd lost their kids and had to struggle even harder than before to find hope, and in some of the most depressing circumstances you can imagine.

When I started rising up in the CLIFF program, I wound up totally embracing the position of helping these women learn about themselves the way I was doing. They made me think about how many people like me are out there, extreme women who need an extra boost of kick-in-the-ass to make the change to save their lives and their families. The system isn't set up to help women like that, and a lot of them get sent straight to prison without even getting to try rehab. I started thinking about what could be changed to stop that from happening, what kind of programs and treatment facilities could be built on the road between addiction, prison, and total self-destruction. The idea grew and grew in my mind, and the more I started getting into managing the CLIFF program, the more I started to think about how I could make something like that happen. I spent a lot of time envisioning the kind of rehabilitation facility that would have helped a person like me, and that would help women like the ones I met in prison, and eventually not just women but addicts in general.

◆

A big part of becoming a stronger person is finding your source of strength. For me, it's Leah. I never experienced happiness until I held my daughter in my arms, and there was nothing I wanted more than to be with her again. That was the biggest driving force in my fight to get out of prison as fast as I could. The second motivation was starting fresh and getting my family back together.

I was working things out with my ex-fiancé. In prison, you have to have someone put money on a phone account for you so that you have minutes to talk. He was putting money on my phone, and we were talking every single day, figuring things out. It seemed like we were doing a pretty damn good job, and I was feeling great about it. We were going to get back together when I got out. By the time I'd been in jail for almost a year, we were talking about where we were going to live. I sent him a thousand dollars to help him get a place for us.

And then one night on the phone I figured out he had a girlfriend.

I didn't cry a lot in prison, but when I did cry, everyone knew it was about Leah or her father. That night I lay in my bunk sobbing so hard my friend had to put her headphones in because it was making her so upset. I was in disbelief. For a year, I'd been putting everything I had into getting out of there because I believed in this hope that I was going to have my family back together. I pushed myself forward thinking about how when I was free I'd have Leah and her father and a house and a family. That was the driving force behind everything I was working for, all the effort I was putting into changing myself. And suddenly it felt like everything I was fighting for had been ripped apart.

Thank god I had come so far already by the time that bomb dropped. That night I was so devastated I could have been down for the count. But I didn't fall apart. I stuck with it. I'd already been in CLIFF long enough by that point that I didn't give up when I was basically told, "Hey, never mind, you don't have a family anymore." It was okay. I was able to keep it together, and that showed me the progress I'd made in myself, that I didn't give up over such a huge setback. And I took that as a major success.

♦

Besides, however betrayed I felt over what happened between Leah's father and me, I still had Leah. She was the most important thing. And unfortunately, a year into prison I still hadn't seen her. I begged her father to bring her, and I don't know exactly why it didn't happen. There were problems with the papers that have to be sent in for visitation. He'd say he sent them, but something would go wrong and he'd have to put new ones in. So I'd send the paperwork to him again. It went on for way too long. But finally, a year after I was locked up, he finally brought Leah in to see me.

That was the funniest day. I was so excited, and everybody on my dorm knew I was about to see her. By that time I'd started teaching the anger management classes and was about to graduate, so I was pretty well known and had some seniority in the community. The day Leah was scheduled to come visit, I had a hundred and thirty women wishing me luck and yelling that they were happy for me as I walked out the door. I still remember coming back from the visit in tears and having a ton of people crowding around asking me how it went. That's the kind of love I had in prison!

Seeing Leah was as amazing as a dream come true. I was so nervous about what it would be like. I'd been away from her for a whole year, and I was afraid she'd be less comfortable around me, or the visit would go bad somehow. But Leah was so excited and came straight for me. My heart just exploded, I was so happy. I have never felt so blissfully happy as when I look at that little girl. She is more than the world to me. The love I have for her and the love I feel for her is the most beautiful thing I've ever experienced, and it's worth everything.

I saw her for a few visits total after that. She was still little but at the age where they grow up so fast, and she was so different and so much smarter every time I saw her. I felt like such a piece of crap having to spend my only time with my daughter in prison, but every minute I had her she'd sit in my lap and I'd just hold her tight. When it was time for her to leave, her facial expressions would kill me. It was so sad. It seemed really clear that she was aware of the situation, that it wasn't good, and that she wasn't going to see her mom again as soon as she wanted. That was extremely tough to stomach.

Still, despite the situation, we had a great relationship and the same amazing bond we've always had.

The family dynamic was as difficult as ever, though. After Leah's father told me he had a girlfriend, he stopped putting money on the phone. I started paying for it, but he stopped answering as often as he did before. And it seemed like every time I called him Leah was either sleeping, or she wasn't there, or she didn't want to talk on the phone. It got to be sort of ugly, and we started talking more sporadically. I remember when I told him about my GED and that I got the highest score, he laughed at me and said, "Yeah, right." He didn't believe me. Whatever. All that kind of thing does is make it feel better to prove a person wrong. I'm over it.

I knew I was getting out of jail if I worked hard enough on the GED. If I got the time cut, I'd be leaving in a matter of months. That's pretty much the best motivation you can have to pass a test. I walked in there thinking, "If I get this, I'm leaving in a month. If I get this, I'm leaving." And when I finally got the time cut, I almost died. I knew I was going to be out in three months. I called my mom and my friends and told them all. But I didn't tell my ex-fiancé. I only ended up telling him a few days before I left, when I had the details, and only because I wanted to see Leah.

◆

Prison turned out to be exactly what I hoped it would be. It wasn't fun, but it gave me the conditions I needed to change. I used that time as well as I could have. I worked my ass off. But there's no perfect success in that situation. Even if I learned to channel all that darkness inside of me and turn it into strength, I know it's never going away. I'm never going to be a regular, chill, easygoing person who never gets mad. I'm always going to have to work to control my anger, and I'll have to keep learning ways to manage my anxiety and depression. That's just a lifetime of hard work that you have to make a commitment to.

I wasn't scare of hard work. But I was scared of getting out and facing my addiction again.

It's a hell of a lot easier to be sober in prison. That was the whole point. Now, before anybody starts to wonder, yes, people do find ways to do drugs in prison. But it's not easy for them to do, and it's nothing like on the outside. Mostly it's the inmates who are on psychiatric medications and trade their meds for commissary or whatever. Which is just about the worst deal you can come up with in general, because then you've got people skipping their meds when they really need them, and then a few desperate addicts zonked out on these serious pills that just turn them into zombies.

I was safe from addiction in prison. But recovery never ends, and I'd be an idiot if I wasn't afraid of the temptation that would surround me when I got out. I knew I was in for a long, hard road.

It was clear one day when we were all watching the news and a segment came on about prescription drugs. The newscaster was talking about how the pharmacies were cutting down on prescription drugs because of all of the abuse going on. They were talking about Vicadin and Oxycontin and they kept showing the bottles and names on TV. Out of nowhere, I started bawling my eyes out. All that was going through my head was, "I'm never ever gonna be able to touch those again in my life."

I don't know how many people understand the feeling. For the first time, I realized I was going to have to live with the feeling of wanting something for the rest of my life, and not being able to have it. Imagine something you really love and want, something you can have any time, and then suddenly someone says, "You're never gonna touch that again in your life."

It's an awful feeling to be so addicted to those pills and know you can never have them again. You feel strong and empowered every day you get through the addition. But it's so pitiful how bad you want it. It's like falling in love with somebody and then losing that person forever, knowing that even if you meet someone else, no one will ever do for you what that person did. I felt like something had died. I cried myself to pieces.

But the feeling was connected to the fact that I was serious about my decision. The pain was proof that I was separating myself from pills and turning onto the road of sobriety. I was putting my new strength into leaving behind those parts of my old life and my old self. It was goodbye.

When I walked out of prison, I was ready to go forward.

12

Thinking About Tomorrow

The faces of family members. The taste of real food. The colors of normal walls and furniture. Everything you ever took for granted in your life jumps out at you when you've just gotten out of prison. And the things you always knew were beautiful are more beautiful than ever.

Reuniting with my daughter that first night out of jail was the most emotional experience you can possibly imagine. There's no way I could ever describe it to you. Just knowing I was going to see her already had me leaping for joy inside, but to have her in my arms and know that from now on I would be able to see her as often as we wanted, it was almost too much for me to handle.

I was so grateful to be with Leah and to hear her voice telling me that she loved me and she missed me. After all those long months in prison, all the bad days I'd spent alone and miserable with nothing but the dream of my daughter to carry me through, I finally had the reward I'd hoped and dreamed of for so long. I had wanted this so bad, to be free and sober in a comfortable, clean place with my daughter in my arms, that when I finally got it, it almost didn't seem real.

The only thing that has ever made me feel complete is my bond with Leah. The only times I remember feeling blissfully happy were the first moment I held her in my arms, and the night I got out of prison and got to have her with me, knowing she loved me. My love for my daughter dragged me back from the edge of death. It pushed me to remember the kind of life I once swore I'd have for myself. It reminded me how important it is to never stop fighting the demons that can threaten a family, whether they involve addiction, depression, anger management issues, disagreements between parents, or something else. Leah deserved so much better than to see her mom and dad yelling and fighting all the time. She deserved better than a mom in jail, or a mom on drugs, or a mom dead. I knew that, and I'd fought to be clearheaded so I could keep that knowledge in my mind forever.

Free time with Leah justifies every struggle I went through to change myself in prison. When we're alone together, there are just the sweetest moments. I cherish the nights we sit together on the bed watching movies, and she talks and babbles in her little squeaky voice about anything and everything. Even when she kind of loses me and I don't have a clue what she's talking about, she thinks it's the greatest thing in the world just to be having that conversation. It's contagious. I love hearing her develop her little catch phrases and quirks. Whenever I ask her something and she doesn't answer, I ask, "Do you hear me?" Now before she answers me she says, "Yes, I heard you!" with the cutest little attitude. She's so smart and funny it just blows me away. When we interact together, everything is special. We'll be hanging out and watching movies and she'll turn around and put her hand on the side of my face, give me a big kiss out of nowhere and say, "I love you." And that just makes me think to myself, "This is why I'm here right now."

It was startling to me at first, how much Leah had grown while I was gone. I don't like to dwell on the time I missed seeing her grow up while I was behind bars. Seventeen months is a long time in a little girl's life. Now she was five years old, already writing her name and picking up hobbies and interests, learning to express her personality. I got to know quickly how smart she was and that she had a real sensitive streak and a need to stick up for people. She won't tolerate you being mean to somebody in front of her. One day I made the big mistake of calling a dog a little fatty. Leah turned to me with total, complete disapproval and said, "That's not nice." She got that sensitivity from her daddy. If you say anything mean about somebody, she will call you out in two seconds. She really cares. We'll have to watch out for her when she gets older, I can already tell. I can imagine her being one of those girls in high school who beats the crap out of bullies, a real Captain Save-a-Kid. I can already see it in her, how tough she is, how goodhearted she is, and how she's turning out. Best of all, I know she can tell how much I love her. She understands her bond with me. I'm very blessed.

Mothers and children should always have a special bond, but it is something that has to be built and cared for. Some people are in prison for such a long time their kids are fifteen years old and absolutely hate them. When families get separated like that, things can get really bad. Kids get taken away from their parents and put with other family members, or if they don't have family members, into foster homes. And when the parents get free, if they ever get free, they have to face all the years they lost building a relationship with their kids. There can be so much anger and hurt. Those are the saddest people I've ever seen, the saddest moments. I saw it so often in prison. I know they want to have that relationship. But the thing is, it's not hopeless. It's never too late. And I say that because of my own experience, because of me and my dad. I went from wishing he would die, hating him, and blaming him for all the sadness I'd felt in my life, and I got to a place where I loved the man and had a close relationship with him. No matter how bad it got, it wasn't beyond forgiveness. It was never too late to get our relationship back.

I was lucky I got my intervention and made my turnaround when Leah was still so young. She was three when I went into prison, old enough to understand a few things about what was going on. She didn't really comprehend everything that happened, but she sort of did. Either way, I actually have a chance to reclaim my relationship with her now that I'm out. I'm lucky enough that I haven't lost near as much as I could have through my mistakes.

♦

I was off to a great start and more determined than ever to show the world how much I had changed. After all, I hadn't changed *everything*. I was still the same person who couldn't back down from a challenge, who liked to prove people wrong. I knew I'd made a huge turnaround in prison, and I knew I'd get the most satisfaction if I blew up everyone's expectations and kicked total ass.

But there were a whole lot of roadblocks to deal with. I

mean, traffic was slow. First of all, I had to deal with figuring out how to have a functional relationship with Leah's father now that I was out and we were going to be sharing time with Leah. That wasn't the easiest thing in the world to do. I was still beyond pissed about the shit he pulled when I was in prison, leading me on and asking for money from me when he had this girlfriend the whole time. And as soon as I was back in the world, I had to deal with his relationship clashing with our plans for Leah's birthday. He didn't want his new girlfriend to feel left out if she wasn't allowed to come to Leah's birthday party, but as far as I was concerned, trying to get me to hang out with his new girlfriend at my daughter's first birthday party after I'd just gotten out of seventeen months in prison was a whole lot to ask of me real fast. We ended up splitting the celebration into two separate parties, so we could just avoid the whole issue.

So that was annoying. But it wasn't as serious as some of the other things I had to deal with. Leah was just old enough that she was able to ask some really tough questions. It was one thing seeing how much older and smarter she'd gotten and realizing how much of that I'd missed. But it was another thing when she said little things that let me know how my time away had affected her. The first night we spent together when I got out, right as we were going to sleep, Leah asked me, "Are you still going to be here when I wake up?"

That ripped my heart open. It just hit me full on with the fact that I had left my daughter alone for so long. Not just for the time I spent in prison, but for the time leading up to it, when I had been so messed up on prescription drugs, so lost in my own mess that I lost my legal rights to her as a mother and was only able to see her as often as other people would cooperate with. I had no way of knowing how much she even remembered of having a normal relationship with me as her mom. From the moment I got that no-contact order and Leah's dad and I were prevented from co-parenting any more, and especially since that led to me signing over custody rights to him, Leah had never gotten to live with me full-time or experience what that was like, having her mom around her in a normal way. She was used to having me leave for two months in rehab or three months in county or seventeen months in prison.

That was not the way I meant for things to go. Having to face the fact that my mistakes had affected her and the way she saw our relationship was extremely difficult. But all I could do was focus on what I had, which was my clearheaded mindset, my sobriety, and my freedom to decide on the right path forward.

Staying clean is the ultimate in "easier said than done." I'm not going to lie. Some days it's very, very hard. For how crazy my life has been up to this point, I have a very boring life now for a twenty-three year old. It's difficult to go from being a girl who goes out all the time and parties like crazy to a girl who lives with her grandparents and never really goes out.

People don't fall for those pills just so they can go to prison and lose everything. No. They do it for a reason that's very hard to give up. The pills trick you into thinking you're living the fast life, living the dream. And they really make you believe it! When they do what you want them to do, pills make you feel like you're exactly the kind of person you want to be, a person without a care or a problem in the world. And pills lead you into situations that seem so exciting and fun and free, glamorous even. They convince you that the parties are the best parties ever, the people are the craziest people ever, and that you're having more fun than most people will ever imagine having. It's intoxicating, and it becomes a love affair, and then it becomes an obsession. Finally it becomes a kind of brainwashing that's very, very hard to unlearn.

It's hard to be twenty-three years old and feel like most of the fun memories in your life are wrapped up in pills. There are no more parties for me. No more hanging out with the kinds of people I used to hang out with, going places where drugs were there for me if I wanted them. The wild lifestyle I gravitated to before was off limits now. What would I do with myself? How would I learn to replace the high I used to get from drugs? The temptation is always there, just behind my shoulder, to abuse pills again. If I'm doing well, I can forget about it. I can keep my mind off of it. But at the same time, I have experienced what opiates do to me, and I can't just forget it completely. As an addict you have to constantly stay focused on all the ways that drugs fucked up your life and the lives of the people who love you. Because if you lose your grip on any of that, the other side of the experience is always there in your mind, waiting to lure you in. And you can never think you're too smart or too strong to fall back into it again. The thing is, you can never escape the fact that you lost your mind on those drugs. You can never be confident that you've erased whatever it was inside of you that allowed addiction to take such a hold on you. It's a constant battle, and some days are harder than others.

But I'm working my ass off, trying to hold onto this. And what makes me completely fulfilled is the love I have with Leah and the emotions I feel when I'm with her. She's really holding onto me, and I'm holding onto her too. It makes me feel like everything is worth something. Leah reminds me every day not just of my responsibilities as a parent and a person, but of the joy I'm capable of feeling. For the first

time in my life, I see the point in everything. I finally believe
I can be happy.

◆

I can't lie: life is pretty boring these days. Not as boring as
prison, but boring. Boredom isn't good. Drugs trick you into
thinking they're going to fill a hole inside of you, but they
leave an even bigger hole behind for you to fill. Finding purpose in my life isn't some spiritual thing I'm doing for fun.
It's literally the only choice I have.

So what's next for me, besides being a mom?

Ever since I was a kid, my life had been defined by depression, anxiety, and addiction. Now, at twenty-three, I finally
have the tools and the self-knowledge to see things clearly for
the first time. Suddenly I can see there are things I'm good
at and things I want to do, talents and interests that I never
paid much attention to before when I was so caught up in all
the bullshit.

That's why the CLIFF program was such an amazing experience for me. For someone who had dropped out of high
school, having that educational environment was amazing.
Right away I was kicking ass in the program, acing my GED,
and taking on as much responsibility as they'd let me have.
The funny thing was that it came so naturally. It made me
think back to the times before I was messed up on drugs,
when I was all about working hard and getting things done.
Whether I was helping Leah's dad study or organizing our
finances, I was always good at staying on top of things and
accomplishing whatever I put my mind to.

I also realized how much satisfaction I took in helping
others succeed. Becoming a teacher and a facilitator in

the CLIFF program, I learned how amazing it feels to be someone people trusted for advice and guidance, and to have the ability to help them. I took so much satisfaction in helping others get through what I'd been through, and it motivated me so much to see their progress. The experience even showed me how I could channel frustration and anger into positive ideas. When I looked around at all the good women who had lost their children to the system, just because they were addicted to drugs and didn't have access to treatment, it made me absolutely enraged. But that anger quickly got me thinking about what I could do to affect that situation.

Now I have a dream I really care about. I want to help other people like me, people who are so strong-willed and stubborn that they need an extreme kick in the ass to help them overcome their addictions. I want to open the kind of facility I started to visualize when I was in prison, a place where people can get the kind of intense blend of education, discipline, and community support that will help them find the strength they have inside.

Just a couple of short years ago, I thought there was no hope for me. I was wrong. There's never a good reason to give up. There's always a way to turn things around. You just have to look at someone like me as proof that it's never too late.

Acknowledgments

I want to say thank you to my family for always being there for me. My mother who showed me strength and love, my father who showed me perseverance, and that it's never too late to change, and my brother who has always shown me loyalty and wisdom. Also my grandma and Grandpa for helping me through my hardest times. I would also like to thank my cousin Krystal for sticking by my side. You are not just family, you are a true friend. Also my sister Candace, who's my guardian angel. Nothing would be possible without you looking over me. And, to Beth Roeser for helping me find the words to speak what was on my mind.

I'd also like to thank MTV for sticking by my side through the hardest times. And last but not least, my managers Nick and Jake and everyone at NBTV Studios. Thank you for all your help and guiding me in the right direction.

Sending love ❤